$24.95 U.S.
$29.51 Canadian

The Mortgage Brokers Guide to Lending

A Real World Guide to Understanding:

*The Credit Application * Loan Programs
*How to get Referrals * Qualifying Borrowers *
*Credit Scoring * Underwriting * Disclosures *
Rate Sheets

And much more for
The Novice *and* Experienced Mortgage Broker

By

Martin T. Koellhoffer

LCCN – 2005938170

ISBN 0-9767968-1-3

Published by

Mortgage Planning Solutions
12306 Winding Woods Way
Bradenton, Florida 34202
www.LearnLending.com

Cover Art by Paula Fitzgerald

Edited by Gloria Koellhoffer

Acknowledgements

It is important that I acknowledge and thank the people who motivated me creatively. It is said that necessity is the mother of invention and I'm here to testify to the accuracy of that proverb. The people with whom I've been professionally associated through the years enabled me to learn the finer points of the Mortgage Lending and Real Estate businesses while honing my proficiency in sales. Some of these people were major positive influences while others were largely negative influences, but without their contributions the concepts and ultimate achievement of this program would not have been possible. In general, their individual methods and attitudes necessitated that I find a way to a more affirmative business approach, driving me to formulate an entirely new program of educating Mortgage Brokers in the fundamentals of mortgage lending.

Tom Cinquegrano; who provided me with an opportunity when I needed one and, together with Chet Horne, helped me learn the essentials of the mortgage brokerage business while giving me guidance and positive motivation at crucial times.

Douglas Rawan, whose vision and foresight inspired me to create my own corporation and its educational division.

Christine, Paul and Mark, whose complete lack of vision and foresight inspired me to create my own corporation and its educational division.

All of the Realtors, Bankers, Certified Public Accountants, and Attorneys that send the continuous referrals of people in need of the creative financing I have become known for.

All of the Bankers, Lenders and Realtors, with whom I've worked throughout the years, who asked me to find a way of bridging the gap between two of the most important professional areas in the business of Real Estate; the Realtors and the Mortgage Lenders.

My family, especially my wife, Filia, and my children, Derrick and Dania, who tolerated the long hours I've spent researching and writing this book, compiling the course materials and rehearsing the presentation, while simultaneously organizing the mortgage division of the company to be immediately productive and successful.

Thank you, all.

Martin T Koellhoffer – November, 2005

Table of Contents

My Background
Our Goal
Referrals – The best source of business
Mortgage Planning Strategies
The Loan Application (1003)
What are note, collateral, mortgage and deed?
Truth in Lending
Good Faith Estimate and other disclosures
RESPA
Understanding the Rate Sheets
P.M.I.
Escrows
Qualifying for a Mortgage Loan
Underwriting the Loan
Types of Property
Types of Loan Programs
The Equity Loan or Line of Credit (HELOC)
Refinance
Rescission Period
Lot or Land Loans
Construction loans
Fixed Rate Loans
Adjustable Rate Mortgage (ARM)
MTA Option ARM
80-20 (100% LTV)
No Income Verification
Foreign National Loans
Non-Conventional & Sub-Prime Loans
Understanding Credit Scoring
Using Equity from Existing Property
Documents Typically Required at Application
The Age of Specialization
Mortgage Banking Glossary

My Background

Since 1977 I have been a consumer finance manager and mortgage loan officer for some of the largest banks and mortgage companies in the Southeast United States. During my tenure as Vice President of the Consumer Lending Division for one of these Banks, I developed a wholesale division to help consumers obtain low cost mortgage loans, using mortgage brokers as a conduit. The principal reason for using mortgage brokers is that research shows 65% of all mortgage loans in the United States originate through mortgage brokers. The success of our wholesale division was immediate and outstanding.

Several of my responsibilities as division manager of these banks was to teach the branch managers and the loan officers about mortgage loan programs, sales techniques, compliance with state and federal laws, and credit score interpretation. At the same time I was also creating new mortgage programs to deal with the rapid growth of the Florida Market.

In 1998, our bank was sold to what is now the largest bank in the United States. To my dismay, the division I had worked so hard to build was to be dismantled immediately following the merger. It was then I decided to become a mortgage broker myself and joined one of Southwest Florida's leading Mortgage Broker Firms as Vice President. While there, I developed a keen sense of the average borrower's needs. I also became aware, and a bit dismayed, of how little the average mortgage broker actually knew about the mortgage loans they were offering.

It was natural to continue utilizing my educational skills with Mortgage Brokers and their clients once I'd made the switch from banking to brokering. I joined the Florida and National Associations of Mortgage Brokers to have access to their wonderful educational programs and currently serve on the Board of Directors of the Southwest Florida Chapter of the FAMB.

In 2004 I wrote and published the book, "Mortgage Education for Real Estate Professionals". I facilitate a bi-monthly class for Realtors, based on the book, at our corporate facilities in Bradenton, Florida. I also write articles about financing for "Real Estate Update" a monthly newsletter that goes out to Realtors.

Recently, I have been working to help develop a procedure for the loan originator to become a team leader and build a team of originators who will then originate their own loans. The team leader will receive an override of commissions from all of his team members.

OUR GOAL

In this book, you will learn:

- The importance of a fully completed loan application.
- What credit scores are, how they are determined and why they are important.
- How to get referrals for loans and how to build your business *fast* by adding other originators to your *own team.*
- The basic information that is required to determine if the borrower may qualify for a loan.
- What a Good Faith Estimate is and when it is required.
- How to understand the differences between various mortgage programs.
- Learn to understand lender rate sheets and adjustments.
- Why people should strategize their Real Estate investment like a stock portfolio.
- How to "cross collateralize" different properties.
- How to use equity from an existing property for down payment without selling it.
- How to find 100% financing *without* PMI.
- Loans with payments that are HALF of what a fixed 30 year loan is.
- Sub-prime lending for people who have major credit issues *and* no down payment.
- How to obtain a "band aide loan" to get into a house now, and then refinance with little or no closing costs in two or three years.
- The difference between No Income, No Ratio and No Documentation loans.
- A complete Glossary of Terms to enable you to understand many of the Mortgage Terms in use today.

The Mortgage Brokers Guide to Lending will help you bridge the gap between the basic licensing exam information you learned to pass the test, and real world mortgage broker lending techniques and programs. Empowered with this information you will have the knowledge and confidence you'll need to effectively assist your clients. By using the Guide as reference, the net result will be more loans approved and closed.

This book is intended to teach Mortgage Professionals the essentials of Mortgage Lending so they will better understand the needs of their clients as they relate specifically to mortgage loans. Once the needs of the client have been determined, it is, of course, essential that the originator know how to structure the loan and where to place it for a successful underwriting approval.
Experienced, knowledgeable mortgage brokers gather essential facts and information that enable them to fully comprehend their client's needs. They also have a comprehensive understanding of the available mortgage loan programs offered by the lenders with whom they have an established, working, relationship. They evaluate their client's needs and then match them with the loan programs offered by a lender that will best meet those needs.

I have made it my personal goal to help educate Mortgage Brokers so they will have as many facts as possible on the basics of mortgage lending. This knowledge will enable them to guide their prospects to an intelligent decision, help choose the mortgage loan program that best suits that prospect's needs, and know how, when, and where, to structure and place that loan. One of the most gratifying testimonials to our service as mortgage brokers is to hear a client say, *"No one EVER explained it to me the way that you just did. Thank you!"* as they sign the application and disclosures for you to begin the loan process. It's been a privilege to have heard this from many borrowers throughout the years.

Many of the consumers I work with are purchasing a new home from a Real Estate Agent. They have been referred to me largely because they have a particular or unusual financial situation. Many of them are self employed or in a commissioned job and can not verify their income. Some are changing careers and do not have sufficient job history in that field to satisfy conventional lender requirements.

Others have cash on hand or tucked away in a box and can not satisfy lender deposit requirements. Occasionally, someone who does not even *have* a job, but may have investments or trust income, needs a mortgage loan. One of my most common challenges involves consumers who have major credit issues and have been turned down by conventional lenders.

By truly *listening* to each client as they express their needs, then evaluating their individual situation with genuine concern to finding a solution, I am successful in placing ninety percent of my loans. It is first and foremost a matter of *understanding* the client's needs. The next step is to have a strong relationship with your investors and lenders and know how to structure the loan so the underwriter will be able to justify an approval.

Many Brokers who deal with a prospect in an unusual or very difficult financial situation will give up on the loan after trying a couple of different solutions. Essentially, this is because they are not aware of the scores of financing options available to their clients from specialty lenders and investors all across the nation. The fact is that 95% of all people who *want* to purchase Real Estate *can do so.* There is no secret to successfully placing a loan. One of the most important factors in qualifying your borrower for a loan, and obtaining a mortgage loan approval for that borrower, is for you, the Loan Originator, to have a fundamental and thorough understanding of the loan programs that are available.

It is important, too, that you be very aware of the lending laws of your state and the federal government's RESPA laws and your HUD closing statement. This will also help to insure that you remain in compliance with the strict state and federal laws that apply to mortgage lending, avoiding the severe penalties that will result for non-compliance.

Our mission is to help educate the Mortgage Broker regarding the enormous variety of loan programs that exist and help them understand how to qualify a prospect for a specific type of mortgage loan.

In my experience I've learned that an important factor in being successful as a Mortgage Broker is to have a comprehensive understanding of mortgage programs and the lenders who offer them. I realize I'm repeating myself on this issue, but it cannot be emphasized enough. Become very familiar with at least two conventional lenders, two specialty lenders, and two sub prime lenders and all of the programs they have available. You'll find that two different lenders will have slight variations of the same programs with slightly different underwriting guidelines allowing one to approve the loan where the other will not. Specialty lenders will have certain programs for strong borrowers that make allowances for no income verification or no documentation loans without requiring a significantly higher interest rate. They will also offer other unique loan programs, such as Option ARMS, high LTV investor loans or low documentation, condo conversion loans. Sub-prime lenders will have programs that will allow for very low credit scores, poor payment history, open, unpaid collections and other credit related issues. Sub-prime lenders will often allow you to use bank statements as proof of income and will consider it the same as a fully documented loan.

Work closely with lender account representatives. Ask them to train you in their particular loan programs. They will be happy to do so if it means you'll be sending them more business. Locate Title Agents and Appraisers you can become familiar with and get to know them so you can trust their judgment and techniques. Allow them to become an extension of your own business. Become a team and utilize your individual experiences, knowledge, and expertise in your own areas of specialization. Additionally, it is crucial to know when it is in your own, and your client's, best interests to call for assistance from your lender-representative for program guidance or clarification. Don't make the often fatal mistake of pretending to know the answers to loan questions. Ask for guidance when necessary. Don't let your ego get in the way of correctly structuring a deal, allowing it to sail through underwriting and close without a problem. Have a working relationship with a reliable title professional that will address, explain and help correct title issues promptly. The same holds true for a dependable appraiser that you can count on for fast service, advice on values, and accurate appraisals that will save you, and your client, time and money.

These working relationships may help to assure that your closing occurs on time. In our business, timely closings, especially when a Real Estate sales contract is involved, is going to give the client, and the person who initially referred the client to you, immeasurable confidence in your abilities.
And remember; never feign an answer to a question or stretch the truth to a client or underwriter. You *will* get caught and then you will have lost the confidence of the people involved, probably your loan, and possibly your license. There is only one way to get a loan through the system; *the right way*.

REFERRALS

The best source of new business

It would be beneficial for you to establish a reliable, working relationship with several Realtors. The Realtor can be a prime source of continuous real estate purchase referral business, and referral business is the best kind of business. The borrower comes to you on the recommendation of someone they already know and trust; the Realtor who helped them to negotiate the purchase and/or sale of their home. At my own company our mortgage division receives from Realtors, an average of 25 referrals that we are able to close each month. Our loan pipeline is always full and there is no more financially comforting feeling than that of a full pipeline.

Realtors are usually the first persons that prospects encounter when they begin looking for property to purchase. It is, of course, the individual Realtor who will either inspire or discourage the prospect's confidence in purchasing and financing a home.

There is much for a Realtor to know when structuring a contract between buyer and seller. They need to know the particulars involving contract negotiations, comparable recent sales, zoning, taxes, schools, businesses, shopping, transportation, and other important issues that are paramount to every buyer. All good Realtors are extremely knowledgeable in these areas. They must be, in order to be successful in their field. It is also essential that Realtors know when to utilize the skills of a licensed mortgage or title professional to help complete the sales transaction. It is fundamental to their success.

By establishing a working relationship with several Realtors and demonstrating to them how your knowledge of financing will help them close more sales, you will assure yourself of a continuous pipeline of purchase money loans. I strongly recommend arranging for monthly training sessions with your Realtors using the program material you will find in my book, "Mortgage Education for Real Estate Professionals" as your training session guide. The book is written to give the Realtor basic understanding of financing so they will be more knowledgeable and, from a loan originator's point of view, easier to work with. It is up to you to present the material in a professional manner. At each training session you will want to offer details on any new or exciting loan programs or techniques that will make them eager to use you, exclusively, to structure and close more purchase transactions.

For example, when the interest only and flex option loan programs first came out, they offered a new way for people to afford a more expensive home. When we brought these new loan techniques to our Realtors they became certain of our genius. Our referrals and closings increased immediately.

Another suggestion is when you stop in to visit a Realtor referral, bring the previous day's rates with you and a print out of a market analysis or market comments. These materials can be obtained on the internet through most of your lenders web sites. Briefly go over them with the Realtors. You will be demonstrating to the Realtor that you follow the market conditions and are familiar with the latest loan programs and market trends. Present the image of an accessible professional at all times. Call them every so often and tell them when rates have gone up or down, just to show you are thinking of them and that you are on top of market changes. Deliver new loan program information in your classes and get the Realtors energized about what *you* can do to help *them* close more sales. Show what information goes on a 1003 and why it is important. Use the chapter on underwriting in my book to show them what an underwriter needs to have in order to approve a loan. As often as possible, demonstrate to them that you are the pre-eminent authority on mortgage financing. Let them know that they should call you any time they have a question, because you will either have the answer at your fingertips, or will be able to find the answer in minutes and get back to them with a comprehensive explanation.

My staff and I make ourselves available to our realtors from 9:AM until 9:PM every day, seven days a week. We don't get called that often at night or on weekends, but it occurs on occasion. A call from one of my Realtors on a Saturday night at 8:45 once saved a deal for that Realtor and I made a $7,000.00 fee income from the resulting loan. It is important for the Realtor just to know that you are accessible should they need you. If you make your hours the same as the Banker or Broker down the street, then you are essentially the same as all the other Bankers and Brokers. You are just another source of loans. You want to be *the* source of the *best* loans and the person that the Realtor can count on to contact when the situation demands immediate attention.

Please note that the above recommended techniques and methods of finding and retaining referral sources have been proven successful by me and the dozens of Mortgage Brokers with whom I have worked through the years.

To obtain information on the subject of how to build your *own* team of loan originators, beginning immediately, please e-mail me at; mtgplan@tampabay.rr.com and put "My Own Team" in the subject line.

MORTGAGE PLANNING STRATEGIES

The concept or idea of Mortgage Planning is to achieve the same goals as when planning any investment strategy. That is, of course, to realize the highest possible return on the investment.

It is unfortunate, but true, that most consumers do not treat their real estate investments with the same consideration and planning that they do on their other major investments. Stocks, bonds, mutual funds, IRA, 401K, employee retirement accounts, and trust funds are given a lot of thought and planning. People spend many hours going over strategies to assure the investment will provide the maximum return. They ask themselves how to best diversify a portfolio. Should it be stocks, bonds, mutual funds or possibly an annuity? What percentage to invest in growth? What about immediate income, and long term stocks? Should they look at municipal bonds or corporate bonds?

Each and every investment decision is given substantial and extensive consideration. For the average person, attempting to organize a portfolio without some modicum of professional guidance is considered imprudent. Even the most seasoned investor needs to consult with a specialist from time to time and, be assured, when they first started investing they consulted with that specialist frequently.

Investment Planners or Financial Planners are essential in assisting each individual to better understand their financial needs and the abilities to meet those needs using available resources. The average person could possibly lose hard earned money trying to build an investment portfolio or manage their own financial programs without professional direction. An investment specialist has a solid understanding of the myriad of programs in the sea of investments and how to best navigate those potentially hazardous waters without running aground.

Typically, the average person at age 40 has about $20,000.00 in an IRA, maybe $40,000.00 in a company 401K and savings of about $15,000.00 if they've planned well. They have spent time consulting with a financial planning specialist and have considered their options for growth and income. With careful planning and a bit of luck they may realize a return on their investments of between six and 8 percent.

Why then, when these same consumers spend $350,000.00 on a real estate investment that will grow at between 15 and 20 percent per year, are they willing to go without any professional investment counseling at all? The average borrower will typically walk into a bank and say, "Give me your best rate on a fixed 30 year mortgage." More often than not, the average loan officer is going to give him what he requests without asking essential qualifying questions. The resulting loan may not be what is best for that individual's needs. By asking the borrower questions with reference to his specific needs and requirements, that banker may have been able to save the borrower hundreds of dollars per month in unnecessary interest. The resulting savings may have enabled him to afford a larger or more desirable house.

Mortgage Planning by a competent Mortgage Broker is to Mortgage Loans what a Financial Planning or Investment Planning Strategist is to stocks, mutual funds, bonds and a 401K. Well trained Mortgage Brokers will help guide their clients to a successful strategy with the largest investment they will likely ever make and show the borrower how they may save tens of thousands of dollars over the life of their mortgage.

One possible way is to explain how an adjustable rate mortgage may be refinanced periodically so that the rate remains between one and one and a half percent lower than a current fixed 30 year rate.

There is no trick to it, just a basic understanding of mortgage loans that will allow you to be aware of what is best in a given situation. Real Estate Investments, whether in a primary residence or an investment property, should be reviewed and adjusted when necessary, just like mutual funds, stocks, bonds and retirement accounts.

In this book you will find many of the fundamental tools that will enable you to help guide your prospect in the selection of an appropriate mortgage loan.

THE LOAN APPLICATION (1003)

The loan application is like a snapshot of the borrower's financial life. It tells us what the borrowers wants are; what the borrowers needs are; their current financial liabilities and assets; their ability to repay the loan should it be approved; and their history of repayment on loans they've obtained in the past.
All of this can be determined by an underwriter if the loan application, the Fannie Mae, Uniform Residential Loan Application,

form 1003, has been filled out correctly and completely by the loan originator.

We are going to go through the application from start to finish, describing what is required to be reviewed, explained, and justified by any and all underwriters prior to the completion of the underwriting process. Please remember, excluding or overlooking any of the required information, whether intentional or unintentional, will cause the loan process to be suspended. You may then have to go back to a borrower, a week or so after they believed you had done your job and completed their application, to ask them for more information. In so doing, you will lower their confidence in your abilities as a reliable loan originator. You will have opened the door to doubt and it is a very difficult door to close again.

Do it right the first time. Fill out the application completely, leave nothing blank, and gather as much information as necessary to obtain a fast underwriting approval.

The following information is primarily from Fannie Mae's documented guidelines regarding the Uniform Residential Loan Application process and more than two and a half decades of personal experience with the 1003 and all of its revisions. Now find yourself a 1003, set it alongside you, and let's go over it page by page. If you cannot find a paper copy, go to: http://www.efanniemae.com, click on "Form 1003" then click on "download interactive PDF" and you'll be able to fill in the blanks right on your computer screen as we go over the 1003.

PAGE ONE

Section I - Type of Mortgage and Terms of Loan

Select and check the box for the appropriate mortgage. Enter the loan amount, the interest rate, number of months and amortization type.

Section II – Property Information and Purpose of Loan

Write in subject property address, complete with zip code. Enter number of units. A single family residence, condo or townhouse would be one unit; a duplex would be two units, etc.

Under legal description, you can enter "see preliminary title report", or enter the actual legal description found in the county property records or on the purchase contract. Enter year built, which can also be found on the county property records.

Be sure that the purpose of loan is filled in. "Other" could be a home equity loan or line of credit. Under Property Will Be, choose a property type: Primary, Secondary, or Investment.

If this is a construction or a construction to permanent loan, fill in the appropriate areas.

If a refinance, complete this section.

Enter the borrowers' names exactly as the title is to be held, then choose the manner in which title will be held.

The "Estate will be held in" field concerns whether the real estate is owned in Fee Simple or is a Leasehold estate. Typically, ownership is in Fee Simple. If Leasehold is involved, remember to enter the expiration date of the lease.

If the transaction is a purchase, select the source of the down payment. Is it from savings, is it a secured loan or from the sale of existing property? Be certain to have documentation as to the origin of the funds.

Section III – Borrower Information

The section is self explanatory; just do not leave any blank spaces. The same will be true of the co-borrower. Check with applicant to verify mailing address is the same as present address. If it is not, then enter the mailing address. Include the Borrower's former addresses if they have lived at the present address for less than two years. If the Co-Borrower has a different former address from the Borrower, be sure to change it, too.

Section IV – Employment information

This section, too, is self explanatory. Do not leave any blank spaces. Be sure to check the "self employed" box if the borrower is self employed. Note that the years on present job may not be the same as the years employed in this line of work/profession. Enter the appropriate time frames for each box. Business title and phone number are essential.
If a Borrower has been employed in his/her position for less than two years, complete the Former Employer fields. If the Borrower has a second or third job, enter that information there as well.

PAGE TWO

Section V – Monthly Income and Combined Housing Expense Information

Enter the primary Borrower's base income. Be sure not to include Overtime, Bonuses, or Commissions, in the Base Income box. There are separate areas for these items. They are to be computed as averages, as opposed to base income. Check with your lender to determine the period over which such income is averaged (usually two or three years).

Dividends and Interest income (Div/ Int) should also be averaged; you can take the figures from the Borrower's tax returns or from bank statements.

Net Rent, if applicable, will be calculated from property information entered later in the Schedule of Real Estate Owned.

Remember to indicate B for Borrower or C for Co-Borrower in the Other Income descriptions. Other income would be social security or disability income, pension, income from boarders, military income, automobile expense account, etc. Other income would then be totaled and carried over to the bottom of the gross monthly income areas.

Combined Monthly Housing Expense: The present monthly housing expenses for the borrower and the co-borrower should be listed on a combined basis. The proposed monthly housing expense for a two- to four-family property in which the applicant will occupy a unit as a principal residence should reflect the monthly payment (PITI) for the subject property. For all one-unit investment properties and all two- to four-family properties in which the applicant will not occupy one of the units, the proposed monthly housing expense should reflect the applicant's principal residence

Section VI-Assets and Liabilities

Check whether this section is being completed by both co-borrowers together or separately (Not Jointly).

In the Cash Deposit section, enter the description of the source of funds and the amount of the cash deposit, if any.

In the "List Checking and Savings Accounts" areas, be sure to enter all requested information on all accounts.

If the Borrowers have stocks and bonds, enter their names and amounts in the Stocks and Bonds areas.

Enter the face amount and cash value of Life Insurance, if appropriate.

Real estate owned should come from the total of the Schedule of Real Estate on Page 3 of the Loan App.

Vested interest in a retirement fund is the dollar amount of the Borrower's pension or retirement to which they have access.

Net worth of businesses owned pertains *only* to sole proprietorships, partnerships, and corporations in which the Borrower has an interest.

Enter the market value of each automobile owned (up to 3) and list any other assets such as furniture, personal property, computers, electronics, jewelry, etc. They can be itemized or aggregated as appropriate.

Liabilities

This section concerns the Borrowers' liabilities. This includes any debts the Borrowers have and any non-housing monthly obligations. If you are filling in this information manually, be sure to enter each piece of information requested, leave nothing blank.

Hundreds of credit companies have built interfaces that allow you to populate the liabilities directly from the credit report to the 1003 if you are using an LOS of any type.

IMPORTANT! Be certain information is entered into the alimony/child support area if applicable.

PAGE THREE
Section VI (cont.)

Section VI of the Loan Application, Assets and Liabilities, concludes with the Schedule of Real Estate Owned. List the details of all properties owned by the Borrowers here.
In the Occupancy Rate field, enter the rate to be used for any rental (non owner-occupied) properties owned by the Borrowers. Lenders typically use 75% as the occupancy rate to calculate net rental income. Be sure to fill in all areas and complete computations.

Section VII-Details of Transaction

This section summarizes the information provided to the Borrower in the Good Faith Estimate, including Purchase Price, Estimated prepaid items and estimated closing costs and the Loan Amount.
The purchase price shown on Line "a" under the "Details of Transaction" should not include any discounts or rebates or other allowances paid or allowed to the purchaser. For refinancing, the amount being refinanced should be shown on Line "d" -- Refinance. The figure should include the total amount of all existing liens plus the costs of improvements that have been -- or will be -- made. Lines

"a", "b", and "c" should not be used to describe a refinance transaction.

Section VIII-Declarations

It is absolutely essential that you personally ask for the answers to each of these questions. They are required by federal law and failure to answer the questions will result in the loan application being suspended by underwriting.

The answers will also dictate many of the underwriting decisions, one of which is; the responses to questions in the Declarations section described below will enable lenders to determine whether an applicant qualifies as a first-time homebuyer. Note that if there is more than one applicant, only one of the applicants has to qualify for first-time homebuyer status in order for the mortgage to be considered a mortgage to a first-time homebuyer.

Section IX and X

This section is included to aid the federal government in monitoring compliance with equal credit opportunity, fair housing and home mortgage disclosure laws. Supplying this information is strictly voluntary on the part of the applicant, but lenders should ask all applicants to provide it, including those who apply by telephone and through the Internet, and should describe the reason for collecting this data. Race and ethnicity are separate categories, and although the lender should ask applicants to furnish information for both, applicants may furnish one but not the other. Note that there is no longer a place for applicants to indicate race as "Other" but applicants may check as many races as apply.

The Home Mortgage Disclosure Act and its implementing Regulation C generally require Lenders to collect sex, race and ethnicity data on all applications.

When an application is taken in person and an applicant elects not to provide some or all of this information, federal law requires the lender to note the applicant's sex, ethnicity, and race on the form, based on the lender's visual observation or the applicant's surname. To aid in identifying applicants who may be of Hispanic ethnicity and who elect not to self-identify, the lender may wish to consult the list of Spanish surnames developed by the U.S. Bureau of the Census. Furthermore, the lender may wish to advise the applicant that he may complete or change the information in this section after the application is approved, at any time up until closing.

To Be Completed By Interviewer

The interviewer must complete this portion of the form to indicate the method used to take the application and to provide the name and telephone number of the interviewer, as well as his or her employer's name and address.

Remember, above all, a *complete* Uniform Residential Loan Application will allow for a faster underwriting time and a smooth closing. If you only have to collect the information from the borrower one time, you will project the professional image that will give your borrower, and referral source, confidence in your ability and help to insure your future success.

QUALIFYING FOR A MORTGAGE LOAN

Qualifying a potential borrower for a mortgage loan is not difficult. It is largely a matter of understanding what the underwriters will be evaluating when determining if the borrower will be able to make the payments on the mortgage loan and if the amount of the loan is in line with the value of the house. These important factors are known as the "ratios." If the ratios are within the acceptable guidelines, most loans can be made.

These are the two ratios that are most important when determining if the borrower will qualify for a mortgage loan:

1. The debt to income ratio, also known as the DTI. The DTI is the total amount of fixed *monthly* payment debt that you have, i.e., your mortgage, any student, auto or other fixed loans, and credit card monthly payments divided by the amount of your total, *gross* monthly income.

For example, if you made $3,000.00 per month and had $1,200.00 in total debt you would take $1,200.00 and divide it by $3,000.00. The final percentage would be 40%. That is your DTI ratio. There are actually two factors within the debt to income ratio. When written, it would be shown this way; 33/38. The first number is your housing, or mortgage expense and the second is your *total* expense, housing PLUS credit cards, car loans, etc. Typically, the debt to income ratio that underwriters consider ideal is the one used in the example above. However, I have obtained an approval when the total expense DTI ratio was as high as *60%.* There can be exceptions made to the DTI rule. They have to do with credit scores, the Loan to Value ratio of the subject property and the borrower's total, *liquid* assets.

2. The loan to value ratio of the subject property is also known as the LTV. The LTV is the amount of the mortgage loan divided by the value (appraisal or sales contract price) of the subject property. For example, if you have a mortgage of $150,000 and the value (appraisal) of the house is $200,000 then you would divide the mortgage amount by the appraised value and the answer would be 75%. That is your LTV.

So, when qualifying, the borrower's DTI and LTV are both taken into consideration and are very important. The underwriters are also concerned with the three "C's". This stands for **Credit**, **Cash** and **Collateral**.

Credit history and credit score are very important. Credit scores can go from a low of 300 to a high of 900. Personally, I've never seen a 300 or a 900. It is important to know that the higher the score, the better the chances of obtaining the mortgage. However, a high credit score alone does not guarantee that the financing will be approved. There are loan programs for almost every credit score, but the best programs with the lowest rates are reserved for the people with the highest credit scores. If your scores are low, then you may still be able to obtain a loan, provided you have asset strength and the LTV isn't too high. We'll cover credit scoring in greater detail later in this book.

Cash is your total income and assets which directly affect your ability to repay the loan. If you have a high DTI, but have liquid assets in savings, mutual funds, stocks, bonds or retirement accounts, the underwriter might make exception to the DTI ratio. They recognize you will be able to obtain money from the asset accounts in the event of an income interruption. You may still be able to get a loan even with NO job as long as you have enough high credit scores, liquid assets and the LTV isn't too high.

Collateral, in the case of a real estate transaction, is the real property itself. If you are trying to borrow 100% on the subject property, then the underwriters are going to want to see strength in other areas, such as credit and income or assets.
In addition, in order to protect their interest in the property with an LTV of above eighty percent, the lender will insist that the borrower obtain, and pay the premium on, Mortgage Insurance.

Qualifying Questions

The following are some of the questions that could be asked of your client to determine their needs. These questions are, more or less, in the order I personally prefer.

Your Broker Principle or Sales Manager may have their own preferences of questions to ask. If you aren't, however, offered that direction, you may consider using the ones listed below. These questions will come following the initial greeting. At the initial greeting you will, of course, give your own name, ask the name and phone number of the client, and the name of the Realtor or other person who referred them to you. In most cases, when it is a Realtor referral, your Realtors should have called you first and given you the essential information regarding the actual purchase transaction. If they have done this, you will already have the answers to many of your questions.

Be sure to have a legal pad on your desk or in your briefcase and have a pen handy to write down the answers to your questions.

For those making a purchase

- Very realistically, how long do you think you'll keep this home? (Can help you determine if a fixed or adjustable rate, or interest only loan will best meet their needs)
- What are you purchasing? Single Family Residence? Multi-Family? Condo? If condo, do you know the percentage of owner occupancy? (Determines what program the borrower may or my not qualify for)
- When do you need to close by?
- Is the property new construction or existing home?
- Are you going to occupy the property or are you purchasing for investment?
- Where is property located?
- What is the sales price?
- How much did you wish to put down? Or, how much of a mortgage are you looking for?
- Have you given any thought to what you want your maximum payment to be, including taxes and insurance?
- How much do you currently pay for rent or mortgage?
- Will the seller be paying any of the closing costs?
- Is any part of your down payment going to be borrowed or given to you as a gift?

- Will there be a co-borrower? Will they occupy the property with you?
- Do you have a copy of your fully executed sales agreement? (If not, and there is a Realtor involved, you can obtain it from the Realtor)
- What is your approximate GROSS income?
- Are you familiar with Credit Scores? Do you know what yours is? (If they don't have a clue, gently ask them "How is your credit? Any problems that you are aware of?")

For those who are refinancing

- Is this your primary residence?
- What type of residence is it? Single family, condo? Multi-family?
- How long have you lived there?
- Very realistically, how much longer do you expect to continue living there? (Can help you determine if a fixed or adjustable rate, or interest only loan will best meet their needs)
- Again, very realistically, how much do you think your house is worth?
- Do you have an existing survey and owner's title insurance policy? (These items could save the borrower hundreds of dollars if they have them)
- What is the purpose of the refinance? (Lower payment, lower rate; get cash out, remodel, etc.)
- Are you self employed?
- Are you familiar with credit scores? Do you know what yours is? (If they don't have a clue, gently ask them "How is your credit? Any problems that you are aware of?")

The above listed questions will help you obtain much of the essential information you'll need to help determine the client's needs. Please remember to ask your Broker Principle or Manager what questions they would prefer you ask before you use the ones in this book.

What are Note, Collateral, Mortgage, and Deed?

Most people are familiar with the noun, mortgage. They believe that this is the document that obligates them to make their payments to a lender. This is not exactly the case. The following examples will help to define the difference between a note and a mortgage.

Note: A written promise to pay a sum of money at a stated interest rate during a specified term. On the following page is an example of a typical Real Estate Note.

NOTE

________________________, _______ _______________________, _______
[Date] [City] [State]

____
[Property Address]

1. BORROWER'S PROMISE TO PAY

In return for a loan that I have received, I promise to pay U.S. $__________________ (this amount is called "Principal"), plus interest, to the order of the Lender. The Lender is ____. I will make all payments under this Note in the form of cash, check or money order.

I understand that the Lender may transfer this Note. The Lender or anyone who takes this Note by transfer and who is entitled to receive payments under this Note is called the "Note Holder."

2. INTEREST

Interest will be charged on unpaid principal until the full amount of Principal has been paid. I will pay interest at a yearly rate of _____________%.

The interest rate required by this Section 2 is the rate I will pay both before and after any default described in Section 6(B) of this Note.

3. PAYMENTS

(A) Time and Place of Payments

I will pay principal and interest by making a payment every month.

I will make my monthly payment on the ________ day of each month beginning on ________________, _____. I will make these payments every month until I have paid all of the principal and interest and any other charges described below that I may owe under this Note. Each monthly payment will be applied as of its scheduled due date and will be applied to interest before Principal. If, on __________________________, 20___, I still owe amounts under this Note, I will pay those amounts in full on that date, which is called the "Maturity Date."

I will make my monthly payments at ____ or at a different place if required by the Note Holder.

(B) Amount of Monthly Payments

My monthly payment will be in the amount of U.S. $____________________________.

4. BORROWER'S RIGHT TO PREPAY

I have the right to make payments of Principal at any time before they are due. A payment of Principal only is known as a "Prepayment." When I make a Prepayment, I will tell the Note Holder in writing that I am doing so. I may not designate a payment as a Prepayment if I have not made all the monthly payments due under the Note.

I may make a full Prepayment or partial Prepayments without paying a Prepayment charge. The Note Holder will use my Prepayments to reduce the amount of Principal that I owe under this Note. However, the Note Holder may apply my Prepayment to the accrued and unpaid interest on the Prepayment amount, before applying my Prepayment to reduce the Principal amount of the Note. If I make a partial Prepayment, there will be no changes in the due date or in the amount of my monthly payment unless the Note Holder agrees in writing to those changes.

5. LOAN CHARGES

If a law, which applies to this loan and which sets maximum loan charges, is finally interpreted so that the interest or other loan charges collected or to be collected in connection with this loan exceed the permitted limits, then: (a) any such loan charge shall be reduced by the amount necessary to reduce the charge to the permitted limit; and (b) any sums already collected from me which exceeded permitted limits will be refunded to me. The Note Holder may choose to make this refund by reducing the Principal I owe under this Note or by making a direct payment to me. If a refund reduces Principal, the reduction will be treated as a partial Prepayment.

6. BORROWER'S FAILURE TO PAY AS REQUIRED

(A) Late Charge for Overdue Payments

If the Note Holder has not received the full amount of any monthly payment by the end of __________ calendar days after the date it is due, I will pay a late charge to the Note Holder. The amount of the charge will be _____% of my overdue

FLORIDA FIXED RATE NOTE--Single Family--Fannie Mae/Freddie Mac UNIFORM INSTRUMENT Form 3210 1/01 *(page 1 of 3 pages)*

Collateral: Property pledged as security for a debt. In the case of default, the lender's claim to that property is exercised to satisfy the debt.

Mortgage: A legal document which pledges real property as security for a loan (note).

The mortgage is the document that connects the collateral, which is the real estate, to the note or loan. When you get a car loan, the car is the collateral. The difference between a loan for a car and a loan for a house is that real estate requires broader legal definition and documentation, hence, the mortgage. The mortgage becomes a part of public record and is recorded with the County in which the real property is located. In effect, the mortgage connects the note to the collateral, or real estate.

On the following page is a typical example of a Mortgage.

After Recording Return To:

____
____
____
____

________________ **[Space Above This Line for Recording Data]** ________________

MORTGAGE

DEFINITIONS

Words used in multiple sections of this document are defined below and other words are defined in Sections 3, 11, 13, 18, 20 and 21. Certain rules regarding the usage of words used in this document are also provided in Section 16.

(A) "Security Instrument" means this document, which is dated ____________________, ________, together with all Riders to this document.
(B) "Borrower" is ____. Borrower is the mortgagor under this Security Instrument.
(C) "Lender" is ____. Lender is a ________________________________ organized and existing under the laws of ____________________________. Lender's address is ____. Lender is the mortgagee under this Security Instrument.
(D) "Note" means the promissory note signed by Borrower and dated __________________, _____. The Note states that Borrower owes Lender ______________________________ Dollars (U.S. $________________) plus interest. Borrower has promised to pay this debt in regular Periodic Payments and to pay the debt in full not later than ____________________.
(E) "Property" means the property that is described below under the heading "Transfer of Rights in the Property."
(F) "Loan" means the debt evidenced by the Note, plus interest, any prepayment charges and late charges due under the Note, and all sums due under this Security Instrument, plus interest.
(G) "Riders" means all Riders to this Security Instrument that are executed by Borrower. The following Riders are to be executed by Borrower [check box as applicable]:

☐ Adjustable Rate Rider	☐ Condominium Rider	☐ Second Home Rider
☐ Balloon Rider	☐ Planned Unit Development Rider	☐ Other(s) [specify] ________
☐ 1-4 Family Rider	☐ Biweekly Payment Rider	

Deed: This is also known as a Warranty Deed or, essentially, the title to the property. This is evidence of the right to, or ownership in, real property. The Warranty Deed is also legally registered with the county in which the real property is located.

The following is a typical example of a Warranty Deed;

WARRANTY DEED

For good consideration, we
(I)____ of
___________________________County of___________________, State of
______________________, hereby
Bargain, deed, and convey to_______________________________of
__________________________, County of
___________________________________, State of _____________________________,
the following described land in______________________________________
County, free and clear with WARRANTY COVENENTS to wit;

Grantor, for itself and its heirs, hereby covenants with Grantee, its heirs and assigns, that Grantor is lawfully seized in fee simple of the above-described premises; that it has a good right to convey; that the premises is free of all encumbrances; that Grantor and its heirs, and all persons acquiring any interest in the property granted, through or for Grantor, will, on demand of Grantee, or its heirs or assigns, and at the expense of Grantee, its heirs or assigns, execute an instrument necessary for the assurances to the title to the premises that may be reasonably required; and that Grantor and its heirs will forever warrant and defend all of the property so granted to Grantee, or its heirs, against every person lawfully claiming the same or any part thereof.

Being the same property conveyed to the Grantors by deed of
__________________________dated______________________, 20____.

Witness the hands and seal of said Grantors, this ____________ day of
___________ 20_____.

Grantor__________________________________
Grantee__________________________________

State of______________________________

County of______________________________

On __________________________before me, ____________________
personally appeared_______________,

Personally known to me (or proved to me on the basis of satisfactory evidence) to be the person(s) whose name(s) is/are subscribed to the within instrument and acknowledged to me that he/she/they executed the same in his/her/their authorized capacity(ies), and that by his/her/their signature(s) on the instrument the person(s), or the entity upon which the person(s) acted, executed the instrument.

Witness my hand and official seal.

Signature______________________________________

Quit Claim Deed: A deed by which the owner of real estate conveys his interest to another but makes no representation that the property is free from encumbrances.

The Quit Claim Deed is typically used when a person or entity who owns real estate wants to add another entity to the deed and title to the land. It is also used in reverse to remove someone from the deed. If a person were to marry and want to add his or her spouse, a quit claim deed would be utilized. Convolutedly, if two people were to be divorced, a quit claim deed would be used to remove one or the other. *BE AWARE* that even if a Judge were to adjudicate that one person receives the real property in a divorce settlement, if both are on the original note and mortgage, *they are both still liable for the repayment of the debt, REGARDLESS of what a judge may have ordered.* The only way out of legal responsibility is to refinance the loan and put it in one name only. The lender will NOT release one person from the obligation despite what a judge orders.

TRUTH IN LENDING (T.I.L.)

The Truth in lending document is designed to show the cost of credit at a yearly rate, the dollar amount the credit will cost, the amount of credit provided to the borrower on their behalf and the amount they will have paid after they have made all payments as scheduled.

This document can be very confusing to the consumer. It is an intimidating form, due to the fact that it contains the total of payments and interest that will be paid over the entire life of the loan, typically two very large numbers. One extremely important disclosure that must be made on this form is the Annual Percentage Rate, or A.P.R.

The APR is calculated using a complex formula. There is no simple technique or formula to calculate it. Ninety-nine percent of bankers could not tell you how it is done. It is important to understand that it must be disclosed. The standard explanation goes as follows:

"The APR is the cost of consumer credit as a percentage spread out over the term of the loan. It includes any charges payable directly or indirectly by the consumer and imposed directly by the creditor as incident to or a condition of the extension of credit. It does not include any charge of a type payable in a comparable cash transaction. Charges that are included in the APR calculation should be indicated as Prepaid Finance Charges on the Good Faith Estimate. Please note that certain items such as Mortgage Insurance Premiums effect the APR calculation directly."

Pre-Paid Finance Charges are certain charges made in connection with the loan and which must be paid upon the close of the loan. These charges are defined by the Federal Reserve Board in Regulation Z and the charges must be paid by the borrower. These charges affect the APR calculation. Each line item on the Good Faith Estimate is indicated with a PFC next to the dollar amount of the item. All items that are to be included in the APR calculation must be noted as Prepaid Finance Charges.

It is important for you, the Mortgage Broker, to understand that the APR will, almost always, differ from the actual interest rate. This sensitive disclosure should be made by a mortgage professional or closing agent so that you are absolutely assured that all state and federal compliance laws have been adhered to. The consequences for non-compliance can be extremely severe. While the above quoted explanation of the APR is acceptable, please get with your Owner/Broker/Manager, or a competent title agent with whom you are familiar, and ask them for an explanation of how they disclose the APR. I have learned some wonderful disclosure techniques from Title Agents and Closers.

On the following page is an example of a Truth In Lending Disclosure.

TRUTH-IN-LENDING DISCLOSURE STATEMENT

(THIS IS NEITHER A CONTRACT NOR A COMMITMENT TO LEND)

Applicants: John Q Public

Property Address:

Application No: PUBLIC

Prepared By: Advance Mortgage Planning Group, Inc.
6150 State Road 70 East
Bradenton , FL 34203
941-782-5551

Date Prepared: 01/18/2005

ANNUAL PERCENTAGE RATE	FINANCE CHARGE	AMOUNT FINANCED	TOTAL OF PAYMENTS
The cost of your credit as a yearly rate	The dollar amount the credit will cost you	The amount of credit provided to you or on your behalf	The amount you will have paid after making all payments as scheduled
* 5.777 %	$ * 276,535.71	$ * 248,681.04	$ * 525,216.75

☐ REQUIRED DEPOSIT: The annual percentage rate does not take into account your required deposit

PAYMENTS: Your payment schedule will be:

Number of Payments	Amount of Payments **	When Payments Are Due	Number of Payments	Amount of Payments **	When Payments Are Due	Number of Payments	Amount of Payments **	When Payments Are Due
		Monthly Beginning			Monthly Beginning			Monthly Beginning
359	1,458.93							
1	1,460.88							

☐ DEMAND FEATURE: This obligation has a demand feature.

☐ VARIABLE RATE FEATURE: This loan contains a variable rate feature. A variable rate disclosure has been provided earlier.

CREDIT LIFE/CREDIT DISABILITY: Credit life insurance and credit disability insurance are not required to obtain credit, and will not be provided unless you sign and agree to pay the additional cost.

Type	Premium	Signature	
Credit Life		I want credit life insurance.	Signature:
Credit Disability		I want credit disability insurance.	Signature:
Credit Life and Disability		I want credit life and disability insurance.	Signature:

INSURANCE: The following insurance is required to obtain credit:
☐ Credit life insurance ☐ Credit disability ☑ Property insurance ☐ Flood insurance
You may obtain the insurance from anyone you want that is acceptable to creditor
☑ If you purchase ☑ property ☐ flood insurance from creditor you will pay $ for a one year term.

SECURITY: You are giving a security interest in:
☑ The goods or property being purchased ☐ Real property you already own.

FILING FEES: $ 146.00

LATE CHARGE: If a payment is more than 15 days late, you will be charged 5.000 % of the payment

PREPAYMENT: If you pay off early, you
☐ may ☑ will not have to pay a penalty.
☐ may ☑ will not be entitled to a refund of part of the finance charge.

ASSUMPTION: Someone buying your property
☐ may ☑ may, subject to conditions ☐ may not assume the remainder of your loan on the original terms.

See your contract documents for any additional information about nonpayment, default, any required repayment in full before the scheduled date and prepayment refunds and penalties

☑ * means an estimate ☑ all dates and numerical disclosures except the late payment disclosures are estimates.

* * NOTE: The Payments shown above include reserve deposits for Mortgage Insurance (if applicable), but exclude Property Taxes and Insurance.

THE UNDERSIGNED ACKNOWLEDGES RECEIVING A COMPLETED COPY OF THIS DISCLOSURE.

John Q Public (Applicant) (Date) | (Applicant) (Date)

(Applicant) (Date) | (Applicant) (Date)

(Lender) (Date)

Calyx Form - til.hp (02/95)

GOOD FAITH ESTIMATE

The Good Faith Estimate, or G.F.E. is a document that, in compliance with the Real Estate Settlement Procedures Act, discloses to the borrower all of the costs associated with the loan transaction. The Good Faith Estimate, or G.F.E., discloses the interest rate and settlement charges in effect on the date of application. The G.F.E. is not required to be issued until an application is actually made. Once the application has been made the G.F.E. must be issued to the borrower within three days following the date of the application. However, if the application is withdrawn during that initial three days then no disclosures are required to be issued.

A misstep commonly made by some Realtors is to obtain a GFE from a lender and attempt to explain it to their client. It is crucial that the GFE be explained by an experienced mortgage professional, preferably the one who has qualified the individual borrower and is able to accurately disclose and define the various loan related fees. Loan scenarios will vary and each borrower's situation is unique. To issue a GFE based solely on a loan amount and note rate is being grossly unfair to the borrower.

For example, if one borrower has high credit scores and can fully document his income and assets, that person should qualify for a very favorable note rate and term. Conversely, if a borrower has low credit scores and is unable to verify his income he will almost certainly have higher rates and less favorable terms. Please be aware that *both* can obtain financing, but their rates, terms and fees may vary greatly. This will, of course, affect the bottom line of the GFE. Understand, too, that underwriting fees are not collective on all loans and may differ by hundreds of dollars. It is important that a loan officer personally qualify each client and ask the questions necessary to provide professional guidance specific to that individual's needs. To do anything less may result in a failure to provide the borrower with all their options, potentially resulting in a loss of credibility and, worse, loss of the sale.

It is also very important to be aware that, once you quote an interest rate to a person, you must also disclose the Annual Percentage Rate. Failure to accurately disclose the APR is a violation of Federal Law Regulation Z. By quoting the interest rate you have represented yourself as a lender and must be duly licensed. If you feel you must quote an interest rate, it may be helpful to quote a range of interest rates and APRs.

The following are almost identical on both the GFE and the HUD statement and, for disclosure purposes, must be completed on the GFE in entirety;

Section 800: Items Payable in Connection with Loan
Section 900: Items Required by Lender to be paid in Advance
Section 1000: Reserves Deposited with Lender
Section 1100: Title Charges
Section 1200: Government Recording & Transfer Charges
Section 1300: Additional Settlement Charges
Total Estimated Funds Needed to Close

Please get with your Principle Broker, Manager, or processor to have them show you the details of filling out a Good Faith Estimate.

On the following page is a typical example of a Good Faith Estimate.

GOOD FAITH ESTIMATE

Applicants: John Q Public
Property Addr:
Prepared By: Advance Mortgage Planning Group, Inc. Ph. 941-782-5551
6150 State Road 70 East, Bradenton, FL 34203

Application No: PUBLIC
Date Prepared: 01/18/2005
Loan Program:

The information provided below reflects estimates of the charges which you are likely to incur at the settlement of your loan. The fees listed are estimates-actual charg may be more or less. Your transaction may not involve a fee for every item listed. The numbers listed beside the estimates generally correspond to the numbered li contained in the HUD-1 settlement statement which you will be receiving at settlement. The HUD-1 settlement statement will show you the actual cost for items paid at settleme

Total Loan Amount $ 250,000 Interest Rate: 5.750 % Term: 360 / 360 mths

			PFC	S	F	PO
800	**ITEMS PAYABLE IN CONNECTION WITH LOAN:**					
801	Loan Origination Fee	$				
802	Loan Discount					
803	Appraisal Fee	(300.00)	✓			✓
804	Credit Report	20.00	✓			
805	Lender's Inspection Fee					
808	Mortgage Broker Fee		✓			
809	Tax Related Service Fee	75.00				
810	Processing Fee	250.00	✓			
811	Underwriting Fee	450.00	✓			
812	Wire Transfer Fee					
	Flood Certification	11.00				
1100	**TITLE CHARGES:**					
1101	Closing or Escrow Fee:	$ 100.00				
1105	Document Preparation Fee					
1106	Notary Fees					
1107	Attorney Fees					
1108	Title Insurance:	1,325.00				
	Search	40.00				
	Exam	75.00				
	Endorsements	135.00				
1200	**GOVERNMENT RECORDING & TRANSFER CHARGES:**					
1201	Recording Fees:	$ 145.00				
1202	City/County Tax/Stamps: Doc stamps	500.00				
1203	State Tax/Stamps: State tax/stamps	875.00				
1300	**ADDITIONAL SETTLEMENT CHARGES:**					
1302	Pest Inspection	$				
	Estimated Closing Costs	4,001.00				
900	**ITEMS REQUIRED BY LENDER TO BE PAID IN ADVANCE:**					
901	Interest for 15 days @ $ 39.9306 per day	$ 598.96	✓			
902	Mortgage Insurance Premium					
903	Hazard Insurance Premium					
904						
905	VA Funding Fee					
1000	**RESERVES DEPOSITED WITH LENDER:**					
1001	Hazard Insurance Premiums 3 months @ $ per month	$				
1002	Mortgage Ins. Premium Reserves months @ $ per month					
1003	School Tax months @ $ per month					
1004	Taxes and Assessment Reserves 3 months @ $ per month					
1005	Flood Insurance Reserves months @ $ per month					
	months @ $ per month					
	months @ $ per month					
	Estimated Prepaid Items/Reserves	598.96				
TOTAL	**ESTIMATED SETTLEMENT CHARGES**	4,599.96				

TOTAL ESTIMATED FUNDS NEEDED TO CLOSE:			TOTAL ESTIMATED MONTHLY PAYMENT:	
Purchase Price/Payoff (+)	250,000.00	New First Mortgage(-)	Principal & Interest	1,458.93
Loan Amount (-)	250,000.00	Sub Financing(-)	Other Financing (P & I)	
Est. Closing Costs (+)	4,001.00	New 2nd Mtg Closing Costs(+)	Hazard Insurance	
Est. Prepaid Items/Reserves (+)	598.96		Real Estate Taxes	
Amount Paid by Seller (-)			Mortgage Insurance	
			Homeowner Assn. Dues	
			Other	
Total Est. Funds needed to close	4,599.96		Total Monthly Payment	1,458.93

These estimates are provided pursuant to the Real Estate Settlement Procedures Act of 1974, as amended (RESPA). Additional information can be found in th HUD Special Information Booklet, which is to be provided to you by your mortgage broker or lender, if your application is to purchase residential real proper and the lender will take a first lien on the property. The undersigned acknowledges receipt of the booklet "Settlement Costs," and if applicable the Consumer Handbook on ARM Mortgages.

Applicant John Q Public Date Applicant Date

As a Mortgage Broker, other disclosures that must be completed, reviewed by the borrower, and signed, prior to submitting the loan to underwriting will typically be as follows;

- Mortgage Brokerage Business Contract
- Equal Credit Opportunity Act
- Servicing Disclosure Statement
- Credit Score Information Disclosure
- Right to receive appraisal
- Patriot Act Identification
- Borrower signature authorization

In addition to the above disclosures, the Federal Government also requires that you send the following two booklets with the appropriate loan programs.

- Buying Your Home Settlement Costs and Helpful Information (To be used on purchase transactions only)
- Consumer Handbook on Adjustable Rate Mortgages (To be used *only* on ARM loans)

These are the most frequently required. There could be more or fewer disclosures required. However, this will be determined by your Principle Broker, Manager, or Processor.

RESPA

The Real Estate Settlement Procedures Act (RESPA) is a consumer protection statute, first passed in 1974. The purposes of RESPA are:

1. To help consumers become better shoppers for settlement services and;
2. To eliminate kickbacks and referral fees that unnecessarily increase the costs of certain settlement services.

Details about RESPA

Corresponding with the above purposes:

1. RESPA requires that borrowers receive disclosures at various times. Some disclosures spell out the costs associated with the settlement, outline lender servicing and escrow account practices and describe business relationships between settlement service providers.

2. RESPA also prohibits certain practices that increase the cost of settlement services. Section 8 of RESPA prohibits a person from giving or accepting any thing of value for referrals of settlement service business related to a federally related mortgage loan. It also prohibits a person from giving or accepting any part of a charge for services that are not performed. Section 9 of RESPA prohibits home sellers from requiring home buyers to purchase title insurance from a particular company.

RESPA in general

RESPA covers loans secured with a mortgage placed on a one-to-four family residential property. These include most purchase loans, assumptions, refinances, property improvement loans, and equity lines of credit.

2. HUD's Office of RESPA and Interstate Land Sales is responsible for enforcing RESPA.

3. **RESPA required disclosures:**

At the time of loan application

When borrowers apply for a mortgage loan, mortgage brokers and/or lenders must give the borrowers:

- A Special Information Booklet, which contains consumer information regarding various real estate settlement services. (Required for purchase transactions only) and
- A Good Faith Estimate (GFE) of settlement costs, which lists the charges the buyer is likely to pay at settlement. This is only an estimate and the actual charges may differ. If a lender requires the borrower to use a particular settlement provider, then the lender must disclose this requirement on the GFE.
- A Mortgage Servicing Disclosure Statement, which discloses to the borrower whether the lender intends to service the loan or transfer it to another lender. It also provides information about complaint resolution.

If the borrowers don't get these documents at the time of application, the lender must mail them within three business days of receiving the loan application.

If the lender turns down the loan within three days, however, then RESPA does not require the lender to provide these documents.

The RESPA statute does **not** provide an explicit penalty for the failure to provide the Special Information Booklet, Good Faith Estimate or Mortgage Servicing Statement. However, bank regulators may choose to impose penalties on lenders who fail to comply with federal law. Please read the section on RESPA enforcement for more information.

Disclosures before settlement/closing occurs

The terms "settlement" and "closing" can be and are used interchangeably.

An **Affiliated Business Arrangement (AfBA) Disclosure** is required whenever a settlement service provider involved in a RESPA covered transaction refers the consumer to a provider with whom the referring party has an ownership or other beneficial interest.

The referring party must give the AfBA disclosure to the consumer at or prior to the time of referral. The disclosure must describe the business arrangement that exists between the two providers and give the borrower an estimate of the second provider's charges.

Except in cases where a lender refers a borrower to an attorney, credit reporting agency or real estate appraiser to represent the lender's interest in the transaction, the referring party may not require the consumer to use the particular provider being referred.

The **HUD-1 Settlement Statement** is a standard form that clearly shows all charges imposed on borrowers and sellers in connection with the settlement. RESPA allows the borrower to request to see the HUD-1 Settlement Statement one day before the actual settlement. The settlement agent must then provide the borrowers with a completed HUD-1 Settlement Statement based on information known to the agent at that time.

The **Initial Escrow Statement** itemizes the estimated taxes, insurance premiums and other charges anticipated to be paid from the Escrow Account during the first twelve months of the loan. It lists the Escrow payment amount and any required cushion. Although the statement is usually given at settlement, the lender has 45 days from settlement to deliver it.

RESPA'S statutes explained: consumer protections and prohibited practices

Section 8: kickbacks, fee-splitting, unearned fees

Section 8 of RESPA prohibits anyone from giving or accepting a fee, kickback or any thing of value in exchange for referrals of settlement service business involving a federally related mortgage loan. In addition, RESPA prohibits fee splitting and receiving unearned fees for services not actually performed.

RESPA does not prohibit an individual from performing multiple settlement services in a transaction. However, there is further scrutiny when that individual is in a position to refer settlement service business, such as a real estate agent/broker. To be paid for providing additional settlement services, the service must be "actual", "necessary", and "distinct" from the primary service that individual provides. Furthermore, any fees received must be "reasonable" in relation to the service(s) performed.

In determining whether the payment is for legitimate services and not merely for the referral of business, the Department will examine certain factors. For example, if a real estate agent is also receiving compensation for so-called mortgage brokerage services, HUD might compare the services performed by the individual with services performed by mortgage brokers who do not perform multiple services; contrast the individual's training and qualifications with those typically required for a mortgage broker; scrutinize any difference in compensation between the individual and mortgage brokers who are not realtors; and examine the way the mortgage brokerage business is conducted, such as whether the individual seeks mortgage business from consumers other than those he is in a position to refer.

Then, HUD would look to see if the compensation is reasonably related to the services performed. If the compensation for services performed were not reasonable, HUD would assume that payment was for the referral of business and not for services rendered, in violation of section 8 of RESPA. Any person who receives unearned fees in connection with a federally related mortgage loan is guilty of violating Section 8 of RESPA, and is subject to both civil and criminal penalties. It is recommended that individuals contemplating the provision of multiple settlement services consult with an attorney prior to doing so, so that they fully understand their legal obligations. It is also recommended that you review Statement of Policy 1999-1 Regarding Lender Payments to Mortgage Brokers as well as Statement of Policy 2001-1 Clarification of Statement of Policy 1999-1 Regarding Lender Payments to Mortgage Brokers.

In addition, it is recommended that you review HUD's FHA regulations as it relates to allowing an individual to perform multiple settlement services. FHA guidelines may not allow an individual to perform multiple settlement services. Within their guidelines, you may be in violation.

Violations of Section 8's anti-kickback, referral fees and unearned fees provisions of RESPA **are subject to criminal and civil penalties.** In a criminal case a person who violates Section 8 may be fined up to $10,000 and imprisoned up to one year. In a private law suit a person who violates Section 8 may be liable to the person charged for the settlement service an amount equal to three times the amount of the charge paid for the service.

Finally, you may want to review HUD's RESPA settlement agreements, which can be found on the Department's, website located at: http://www.hud.gov/offices/hsg/sfh/res/respa_hm.cfm Specifically, HUD reached a settlement agreement with a company, Znet Financial, which paid realtors for so-called origination services.

Section 9: Seller required title insurance

Sec. 2608. Title companies; liability of seller

(a) No seller of property that will be purchased with the assistance of a federally related mortgage loan shall require directly or indirectly, as a condition to selling the property, that title insurance covering the

property be purchased by the buyer from any particular title company.
(b) Any seller who violates the provisions of subsection (a) of this section shall be liable to the buyer in an amount equal to three times all charges made for such title insurance.

(b) (Pub. L. 93-533, Sec. 9, Dec. 22, 1974, 88 Stat. 1728.)

RESPA enforcement

Civil law suits

Individuals have one (1) year to bring a private law suit to enforce violations of Section 8 or 9. A person may bring an action for violations of Section 6 within three years. Lawsuits for violations of Section 6, 8, or 9 may be brought in any federal district court in the district in which the property is located or where the violation is alleged to have occurred.

HUD, a State Attorney General or State insurance commissioner may bring an injunctive action to enforce violations of Section 6, 8 or 9 of RESPA within three (3) years.

Filing a RESPA complaint

Persons who believe a settlement service provider has violated RESPA in an area in which the Department has enforcement authority (primarily sections 6, 8 and 9), may wish to file a complaint. The complaint should outline the violation and identify the violators by name, address and phone number. Complainants should also provide their own name and phone number for follow up questions from HUD. Requests for confidentiality will be honored. Complaints should be sent to:

Director, Office of RESPA and Interstate Land Sales
US Department of Housing and Urban Development
Room 9154
451 7th Street, SW
Washington, DC 20410

UNDERSTANDING THE RATE SHEET

Typically you will receive rate sheets from your various lenders once a day. They will arrive by either fax or e-mail or you may have to go to the lenders web site and look them up. What ever the method of delivery, they will almost always appear in the same format. Learning to understand the rate sheet is vital to your transaction being profitable. Your borrower will want the best rate, under the circumstances. You will want to give that borrower the best rate possible while making as much profit as you can, under the circumstances.

The two most important factors on the rate sheets that need to be understood are the Rate and the Price. The rate is the actual interest rate that the borrower will pay the lender on the loan. The price, also known as the Yield Spread Premium, is what the lender will pay you for originating the loan. This is your profit. There are, however, additional considerations on the rates sheets that will lead to the final rate and price. These are known as the adjustments.

The following is an example of a typical rate sheet.

On the far left hand column you'll see the interest rate. The "15", "30", and "45" Day numbers indicate how many days that rate can be locked for and still hold the same pricing. The numbers that are *IN* parentheses under the "Days" are YSP (profit) or what the lender will pay you for originating the loan. The numbers that are *NOT* in parentheses are what you have to *pay* the lender to get the interest rate shown.

As you can see, the conforming 30 year fixed at 6.125 is paying YOU .351 percent for a 30 day lock. Therefore, if the loan amount were $100,000 your profit would be $100,000 X .351% = $351.00 in profit paid by the lender to you. It is, of course, between you and the borrower as to what interest rate you settle on.

CONFORMING CONVENTIONAL

CONFORMING 30YR FIXED				CONFORMING 20YR FIXED			
60D lock add		0.25	to 30D	60D lock add		0.25	to 30D
RATE	15 DAY	30 DAY	45 DAY	RATE	15 DAY	30 DAY	45 DAY
5.375	2.922	3.016	3.141	5.500	2.235	2.329	2.454
5.500	2.325	2.419	2.544	5.625	1.666	1.760	1.885
5.625	1.759	1.853	1.978	5.750	1.227	1.321	1.446
5.750	1.179	1.273	1.398	5.875	0.766	0.860	0.985
5.875	0.630	0.724	0.849	6.000	0.253	0.347	0.472
6.000	0.093	0.187	0.312	6.125	(0.218)	(0.124)	0.001
6.125	(0.445)	(0.351)	(0.226)	6.250	(0.456)	(0.362)	(0.237)
6.250	(0.840)	(0.746)	(0.621)	6.375	(0.902)	(0.808)	(0.683)
6.375	(1.359)	(1.265)	(1.140)	6.500	(1.306)	(1.212)	(1.087)
6.500	(1.790)	(1.696)	(1.571)	6.625	(1.571)	(1.477)	(1.352)
6.625	(2.158)	(2.064)	(1.939)	6.750	(2.042)	(1.948)	(1.823)
6.750	(2.387)	(2.293)	(2.168)	6.875	(2.418)	(2.324)	(2.199)
6.875	(2.802)	(2.708)	(2.583)	7.000	(2.649)	(2.555)	(2.430)

CONFORMING 3/1 TREASURY 2.750 Margin; 2/2/6 caps				CONFORMING 5/1 TREASURY 2.750 Margin; 5/2/5 caps			
60D lock add		0.156	to 30D	60D lock add		0.156	to 30D
RATE	15 DAY	30 DAY	45 DAY	RATE	15 DAY	30 DAY	45 DAY
5.125	1.800	1.894	1.987	5.000	1.953	2.078	2.171
5.250	1.378	1.472	1.565	5.125	1.479	1.604	1.697
5.375	1.021	1.115	1.208	5.250	1.007	1.132	1.225
5.500	0.666	0.760	0.853	5.375	0.539	0.664	0.757
5.625	0.377	0.471	0.564	5.500	0.138	0.263	0.356
5.750	0.092	0.186	0.279	5.625	(0.259)	(0.134)	(0.041)
5.875	(0.156)	(0.062)	0.031	5.750	(0.585)	(0.460)	(0.367)
6.000	(0.367)	(0.273)	(0.180)	5.875	(0.902)	(0.777)	(0.684)
6.125	(0.601)	(0.507)	(0.414)	6.000	(1.174)	(1.049)	(0.956)
6.250	(0.824)	(0.730)	(0.637)	6.125	(1.429)	(1.304)	(1.211)
6.375	(1.006)	(0.912)	(0.819)	6.250	(1.667)	(1.542)	(1.449)
6.500	(1.149)	(1.055)	(0.962)	6.375	(1.793)	(1.668)	(1.575)

The following page shows just a few of the “adjustments” that may affect the *interest rate*. The adjustments must be either added to, or subtracted from, the rate. The rate sheet will tell you which to do. You should meet with your manager to discuss the rate sheets and how they are applied in your company until you are competent, absolutely certain, and able to calculate it on your own. In the case of rate and margin, when the adjustment *IS IN* parentheses you would *lower* the rate and margin. When it is *NOT* in parentheses, you would *add* it to the rate and margin. (The definition of margin is covered later in the book under the adjustable rate loan category)

Risk Based Adjustments (rate and margin)	
LTV <=70% Primary or 2nd Home	(0.125)
LTV >80% - 85% Primary or 2nd Home	0.375
LTV >85% - 90% Primary or 2nd Home	0.375
LTV >90% - 95% Primary	0.750
LTV <=80% Investment	0.375
LTV >80% - 85% Investment	1.000
LTV >85% - 90% Investment	1.125
Cashout Refinance	0.125
100% TLTV (Available only on Stated Income w/VOA)	0.000
Multi-Family 3, Multi-Family 4	0.250
Interest Only	0.500
Document Type Adjustments (rate and margin):	
No Doc	0.625
Stated Income/Stated Asset	0.375
Stated Income/Verification of Assets	0.250
Stated Reduced	0.625
No Ratio/Stated Asset	0.500
No Ratio/Verification of Assets	0.375
FICO Score Adjustments (rate and margin):	
>=700	0.000
620-699	0.125
Prepayment Adjustments (rate and margin):	
2 YR Prepayment	(0.375)
3 YR Prepayment	(0.500)
* 3 YR Prepayment n/a on 2/28 ARM Note: Maximum YSP (SMC) with prepay = (3.000)	

In the examples below, the adjustments are to the *pricing*. (Your profit) When the adjustment *IS IN* parentheses, you would *ADD* that amount to your pricing. (Profit) When it is *NOT* in parentheses, you would *SUBTRACT* it from your pricing. When it is being subtracted this is also known in the mortgage world as a "hit" to your pricing, or reducing your profit.

3/1 LIBOR ARM
2.250 Mgn; 2/2/6 Caps

60D lock add		0.125	to 30D
RATE	**15 DAY**	**30 DAY**	-
6.000	0.587	0.712	
6.125	0.242	0.367	
6.250	(0.098)	0.027	
6.375	(0.370)	(0.245)	
6.500	(0.634)	(0.509)	
6.625	(0.826)	(0.701)	
6.750	(1.038)	(0.913)	
6.875	(1.241)	(1.116)	
7.000	(1.433)	(1.308)	

5/1 LIBOR ARM
2.250 Mgn; 5/2/5 Caps

60D lock add		0.125	to 30D
RATE	**15 DAY**	**30 DAY**	-
5.750	0.928	1.053	
5.875	0.453	0.578	
6.000	0.045	0.170	
6.125	(0.358)	(0.233)	
6.250	(0.692)	(0.567)	
6.375	(0.988)	(0.863)	
6.500	(1.275)	(1.150)	
6.625	(1.584)	(1.459)	
6.750		(1.728)	

3/1 Treasury ARM
2.750 Mgn; 2/2/6 Caps

60D lock add		0.125	to 30D
RATE	**15 DAY**	**30 DAY**	-
5.875	0.398	0.523	
6.000	0.058	0.183	
6.125	(0.213)	(0.088)	
6.250	(0.478)	(0.353)	
6.375	(0.670)	(0.545)	
6.500	(0.851)	(0.726)	
6.625	(1.053)	(0.928)	
6.750	(1.245)	(1.120)	
6.875	(1.399)	(1.274)	

5/1 Treasury ARM
2.750 Mgn; 5/2/5 Caps

60D lock add		0.125	to 30D
RATE	**15 DAY**	**30 DAY**	-
5.750	0.928	1.053	
5.875	0.453	0.578	
6.000	0.045	0.170	
6.125	(0.358)	(0.233)	
6.250	(0.692)	(0.567)	
6.375	(0.988)	(0.863)	
6.500	(1.275)	(1.150)	
6.625	(1.584)	(1.459)	
6.750		(1.728)	

P.M.I
(Private Mortgage Insurance)

Also know as M.I. (mortgage insurance), this is insurance that the lender will require on most loans if the Loan to Value (LTV) on the first, or primary, mortgage exceeds eighty percent of the value of the subject property. There are mortgage loans available that will actually provide funds for up to 103% of the value of the property being purchased. However, any mortgage loan over 80% LTV requires Mortgage Insurance, or what some people know as PMI. (Private Mortgage Insurance) Mortgage insurance is mandatory on all Fannie Mae, Freddie Mac, and most loans when the LTV is at any level at or above 80.01%. The reason for this is historical. Most houses taken back in a foreclosure are resold for approximately 80% of their value. When the repossessed property is sold this way it is called a distress, or foreclosure sale. The Mortgage Insurance Company pays the difference on what the house actually sells for and the outstanding balance of the mortgage, so the lender isn't forced to suffer a loss. On average, M.I. is going to add approximately $100.00 per month to the payment on a $250,000 mortgage. The higher the loan amount, the higher the premium on the Mortgage Insurance. Later in this book we will show you how obtain up to 100% financing and not have to pay Mortgage Insurance.

ESCROWS

The escrow is the amount of money that is collected and held each month by the lender or loan servicer to pay taxes and insurance premiums. It is typically calculated annually, the sum total of which is divided equally over twelve months and collected along with the principle and interest payment every month. The monies are set aside in an escrow account and paid according to the schedule set forth by the local tax office and individual insurance companies when they become due. This way, the lender is assured that the taxes and insurance premiums will be paid on time.

Many lenders will allow an individual to pay his own taxes and insurance as an option, depending on the total Loan to Value which they prefer to be no more than eighty-percent. However, because the lender cannot be absolutely certain that the payments will be made on time, or at all, this increases the risk factor on the loan. There is frequently a premium charged for this increased risk factor of up to twenty-five basis points or one quarter of one percent.

UNDERWRITING THE LOAN

It is essential that you have at least a basic understanding of what the underwriter of a mortgage loan must evaluate, so you will understand why certain documentation is required of the borrower.

A fully documented loan, which is the loan program that will get the borrower the best interest rate and term, requires the following:

1. If they are **salaried:** provide two years W-2 and one month of pay stubs **OR** if they are **self-employed**: provide two years tax returns and a YTD profit and loss statement.
2. If they own rental property, provide rental agreements and two years tax returns.
3. If they wish to speed up the approval process, also provide three months bank statements for each bank, stock and mutual fund account.
4. Provide recent copies of any stock brokerage or IRA/401K accounts that they may have.
5. If they are requesting cash out refinancing, provide a letter explaining what they plan to do with the proceeds.
6. Provide a copy of divorce decree if applicable.
7. If they are NOT U.S. citizens, provide a copy of their green card (front & back) or, if they are NOT permanent residents provide their H-1 or L-1 Visa.

The best rates and terms generally come from a Fannie Mae or Freddie Mac loan program. This means the underwriter must determine if the loan meets the qualifying guidelines for sale in the secondary market. (See Mortgage Banking Glossary) In order to meet these guidelines the loan must contain certain, very specific and well documented information. It is the underwriter's job to extensively review that file in order to guarantee, absolutely, that all of the documentation requirements have been met.

The underwriter must review the bank statements, making certain that they are complete and that all pages of the statement have been included and that no unusually large deposits have been made recently. This is to assure that the funds are all coming from a reliable income source. The exception to this rule would be if the deposit is coming from the recent sale of Real Estate or some other large asset. The underwriter would then need to see evidence in the form of a HUD from the sale of property or a receipt of sale involving any other large asset.

They would also need to verify income and employment using W-2's or tax returns and review these documents for accuracy and authenticity. (There have been instances where a borrower has forged these documents in an attempt to obtain financing.) It is probable an underwriter will verify employment and the likelihood of continued employment by contacting the employer directly or by requiring a written, or verbal, Verification of Employment (VOE) from the originator or loan processor. With a self employed borrower they may require a copy of a business license or a letter from a CPA verifying two years in business as a self employed individual. Should a person be employed for less than two years, they may require documentation from a previous employer verifying employment, such as previous pay stubs, tax returns, or a VOE.

In the event of a purchase, the sales contract will be reviewed by the underwriter. It must be fully executed (signed by all parties involved in the purchase and sale) and must contain any contingencies and/or seller paid concessions. (Seller paying closing costs) It is important that you, as the loan originator, review the contract in it's entirety to assure that everything that should be in the contract is accurate, true and correct. Typically, furniture cannot be a part of a Real Estate sale. It must be separated and priced out on an addendum and not included in the purchase price of the Real Estate itself. Fannie

Mae will not make allowances for the financing of furniture. Please get with your manager should this situation arise.

The underwriter must also review the appraisal of the subject property to guarantee that all of the comparables used are within acceptable guidelines and the value of the subject property is within market guidelines. It is important to be aware that comparables are based on SOLD properties, *not* listed properties. They must be within the same neighborhood if possible or, if no recent sales exist within the same neighborhood, the comparison must be from the next available neighborhood closest in geographical proximity to the subject property. The comparable property must be of equivalent square footage, age, type of construction and contain similar amenities. If not exactly comparable, the appraiser must make adjustments that are realistic in scope and document these adjustments as percentages.

Should the underwriter believe that the appraisal does not fall within acceptable guidelines, they could order a review appraisal by another professional, state licensed appraiser, which the borrower must pay for. Should the review appraiser disagree with the original appraised value, the underwriter will lower the loan amount based on the subject property not meeting the valuation standards. Should that occur, the borrower *may* have the option to put up the difference *in cash* between the determined appraised value and the contract price and still close the transaction.

TYPES OF PROPERTY

It is important to understand the differences between the various types of properties.

1. Single family residence
2. Town home
3. Condominium
4. Mobile Home (with and without land)
5. Multi family

6. Second or vacation home
7. Income or Investment property (typically a rental property with less than 4 units
8. Commercial property

The average person is going to be purchasing a single family home as their primary residence. This type of property is where they will be able to obtain the best rates and terms.

A Town Home is the same as a single family residence unless it is a town home with zero land lines, then it may be considered a condominium.

A Condominium may also be a primary residence but if it is more than four stories high it is considered a "high-rise" and there is generally a rate adjustment added to the base interest rate. There may be other adjustments depending on the lender. Some have an added charge to the rate regardless of the height of the condominium.

Mobile homes are unique. A mobile home without land is considered the same as an automobile or a recreational vehicle. It has a vehicle title just like an automobile. A mobile home with land is given greater consideration, but is still restricted by most lenders who are willing to make a loan on it.

A multi family home is anything from a duplex to a four plex. The rates, loan types and terms for a duplex may be the same as a single family home, unless it is solely for an investment and will be fully rented. If one side of the duplex is the buyer's primary residence, then the entire property will be considered by the underwriters as primary residence.

There are typically higher rate adjustments for three and four family homes regardless of whether one of the units may be the primary residence of the borrower. Anything above a four family building is considered commercial property and the loan will then be qualified and closed as a commercial loan with rates and terms being set according to commercial loan guidelines.

Second homes or vacation residences may, depending on circumstances, be considered the same as a primary residence regarding rates and terms. Typically, there is a slightly higher interest rate adjustment for second homes. If the buyer cannot verify that the property is their primary or secondary residence, it is classified as investment property and the rate will be adjusted accordingly. Be aware that there are geographical restrictions regarding second and vacation homes. Generally, the second home must be located more than 50 miles from the primary residence; however, the distance requirements may vary between lenders.

Income, or investment property, can be anything from a single family residence to a four family unit. This is property which is being purchased solely for the purpose of renting it for income or future capital gain. The requirements for this type of loan differ from lender to lender. Often, investors are unable to verify part or all of their income. In many instances it is possible to obtain a mortgage loan on a stated income basis for investment properties. Most stated income investment property loans have a limited LTV. Whether or not this type of loan will be workable depends on the skill of the person structuring the mortgage loan.

Residential property that has over four units per building, or more than four residential units per deeded property, is considered commercial. Of course, an entire apartment house, a warehouse, a condominium office in a strip mall, the entire strip mall, a free standing building zoned commercial, a multi-story office building or anything of that nature would be commercial property. There are many ways to structure a commercial loan. It is, of course, important to have a relationship with a commercial lender. Then, it would depend upon the skill and experience of the mortgage specialist structuring the loan to determine if it could be successfully underwritten.

BE AWARE OF PROPERTY "FLIPS"

There are certain geographical regions where property appreciation is out-pacing the rest of the country and many people are purchasing properties with the intention of "Flipping" them for profit. This means that they intend to buy the property, using a residential mortgage, and sell it within a few months or immediately after taking possession. Florida property values are currently appreciating at a rate of more than thirty percent per year on average. This means that a house that sold for $300,000.00 in January, could conceivably sell for $322,500.00 in March of the same year. Of course, this means that a seller could potentially make a considerable profit very quickly, but at the expense of the lender holding the note and mortgage.

A residential loan is made with the lender counting on making a certain amount of interest profit. Typically, it costs the lender more than a thousand dollars to originate that loan. The loan must be set up for servicing, documents must be prepared and shipped and there are other overhead and expense costs. In order for the lender to realize the essential profit to remain in business, the loan must be retained for approximately one year.

Currently in the world of Real Estate financing many lenders are beginning to crack down on those who are taking advantage of residential Real Estate Mortgage loans to purchase and flip investment properties. Residential loans were created to help the average person purchase a primary residence or second home. If an underwriter sees the subject property was recently purchased and is being re-sold at a much higher price, they may consider it a flip and deny the loan. Lenders do not want to extend a residential mortgage loan on a property that is being flipped for profit or encourage the practice in any way.

Please be aware if a Realtor is selling a property that is being "Flipped" the prospective buyer could have a problem obtaining a mortgage loan. Structure the application accordingly and submit it to an appropriate lender who allows for no seasoning (no minimum time of possession) financing on flip properties.

TYPES OF LOAN PROGRAMS

The vast array of loan programs that are available to consumers is staggering, and there are often many different ways to structure the same loan. The following are the most common loan programs;

- There is the old stand-by, the fixed thirty year loan. In today's modern world of conventional mortgage lending, this is typically the loan with the highest interest rate.
- The new FORTY-YEAR AMORTIZATION loans. This longer amortization period will give a lower payment than the thirty-year loan at the same interest rate.
- There is the fixed fifteen year loan where the interest rate may be one half percent lower than the thirty-year fixed rate. This can save the borrower tens of thousands of dollars in interest over the loan term but the payment will likely be higher than the thirty-year payment.
- There are hybrid adjustable rate loans that have the first one to ten years of their term at a fixed rate before they become adjustable. There are also loans that begin adjusting immediately.
- There are loans that give up to three different payment options each month, one of those leading to potentially negative amortization, but offer some very low payment options.
- Sub-prime loans that are designed to help people with minor, or even major, credit issues afford to purchase a home.
- Several types of loans will help self employed people obtain a mortgage when they have been in business only a short time or cannot verify their income.
- There are loans to help people who have little or even no money to put down or go towards closing costs.
- There are loans to purchase a piece of raw land, whether it is a single lot for the borrowers own home or to develop up to ten acres for a single estate home.
- There are construction loans that enable a person to build a house literally from the ground up.
- There are also loans that will allow a borrower to use the equity in their home on a revolving basis, which could be for home improvements, their child's college education, debt consolidation or to make an investment in anything they wish.
- Then, of course, there are commercial loans to buy a business, start a business, construct a building for an existing business or obtain a line of credit on a business.

The primary ingredient for the success of all of the above mentioned mortgage loan programs is knowing where to look for the appropriate lender and how to best structure the mortgage loan to meet the borrower's needs and obtain underwriting approval.

If an application is structured incorrectly, an underwriter may turn down the loan. If that same loan is restructured correctly and sent back to the very same underwriter it could be approved.

Understanding the type of loan that would best serve the borrower's needs and knowing how to properly structure that loan will make the difference between having an application turned down and a quick, clean approval and closing.

THE EQUITY LOAN OR LINE OF CREDIT

The HELOC, or Home Equity Line Of Credit, is a very useful financial tool. The HELOC can be used for investments, home improvements, debt consolidation, education or vacations and, most importantly, a down payment on another property. One reason to use a HELOC is that the interest is tax deductible as long as the collateral is the primary residence. Many people use the HELOC to make investments in stocks or bonds, business opportunities and income properties. As a rule, it is very simple to obtain. Provide a standard loan application and, as long as the credit is good, they could qualify for up to 80% LTV at a very attractive interest rate. They may qualify for up to 100% LTV, but the interest rate could be considerably higher than at 80%. Some lenders will allow them to obtain up to 80 or even 90% of the property value without any documentation at all. If the loan amount is under $200K, they may also be able to avoid having to purchase title insurance. Simply a good credit score and credit history may get the job done. Finding these programs is the mission of an experienced, professional, mortgage loan officer, one with the industry contacts to successfully place the loan.

The CLTV, or Combined Loan to Value, is the amount of the new HELOC and the first mortgage combined. In other words, if the property is worth $100K and the first mortgage is $50K the borrower would qualify for a HELOC of $30K or 80% CLTV. With verification of income and assets, they may qualify for up to one hundred percent.

The HELOC is particularly effective when used as down payment for a new home purchase. Since most HELOC's are interest only, the borrower may use the funds for a down payment on a Real Estate purchase. Then, when they list their existing house for sale, they need only make the interest payments on the HELOC until the house sells. Interest only payments are characteristically lower than fully amortized loan payments. When their current house sells, they use the proceeds from that sale to pay off the HELOC. It is essentially using the equity in their current home before it's been sold instead of after in order to purchase a new home.

REFINANCE

There are a number of reasons why a person may want to refinance an existing mortgage loan. One would be if interest rates had dropped far enough below the rate on the existing mortgage that it became prudent to refinance for a lower rate and payment or to shorten the term. Another would be to lower the rate and possibly pull out cash for an investment or down payment on another property. Some mortgage companies have a program where once the client has obtained a mortgage and paid the closing costs, they won't have to pay them again if they refinance with the same company on the same house. This can amount to thousands of dollars in closing cost savings for the client, and an assurance of repeat business for the Mortgage Broker. Get with your manager to find out how to show a loan with little, or no, closing costs.

RESCISSION PERIOD

A rescission period is the three business days after the date the borrower signs the refinance or HELOC documents, a federally required "cooling off" period. The federal government determined that when an individual is using their primary residence as collateral for a refinance or home equity loan, they must wait three business days after signing before they are fully committed and obligated to the loan. In other words, if they were to refinance their home, or obtain a HELOC, and sign the documents on Monday, they would have to wait until that Friday before the funds are available and they are fully obligated and may use the funds. Should they decide during that period that they have changed their mind and no longer wish to have that loan, they would sign a document called a "rescission form", submit it to the lender no later than midnight of the night prior to the funding day and the loan is rescinded and cancelled. If this provision is executed there is no obligation to the consumer what-so-ever. Should they not rescind by that deadline, then the funds are available and the loan begins accruing interest from the date that they signed the original documents.

LOT or LAND LOANS

A lot, or land loan, is a loan for undeveloped, raw land. Most often, the interest rates on these loans are higher than they would be on the same property with a dwelling on it. The reason for this is that the land by itself has limited value and, historically, people will give up this loan first should they fall on hard times. Most people purchase a lot with the intention of building a house on it in the near future. Some purchase it with the intention of reselling it for a profit. The use of it doesn't matter in the case of a lot loan. However, most lot loans are given a limited term and then balloon out. The typical term is three to five years and then the loan must be refinanced or a house must be under construction on the lot.

Another way of obtaining a lot loan is to combine it with a construction loan. Many lenders will allow you to purchase a lot simultaneously with a loan for construction, even if the lot purchase and construction contract involve two different entities. This is advantageous for people who wish to purchase the lot from one party, and contract a builder separately for the construction yet close simultaneously with the intention of starting construction shortly thereafter. There are several advantages to this scenario;
One, there is only one closing, circumventing the closing costs of two separate loans.
Two, the interest rate will be less because it is based on the property with a dwelling on it and not raw land.

Three, all of the funds come from one source and there is only one payment.

CONSTRUCTION LOANS

Construction loans are a loan that is obtained for the purpose of building a home or commercial building from the ground up. It could also be for the refurbishing or rehabilitation of an existing building. The funds are dispersed to the builder in draws. It is usual and customary for the builder to receive ten percent at closing in order to begin the construction. Then, as the builder completes each phase of the construction, he requests additional draws to continue the work. The lender will send an inspector out to ascertain that the builder has completed the previous phase and, upon receiving a satisfactory report from the inspector, will issue the draw check for the next phase. Typically, there are five phases of construction and five draws. The final ten percent is held until the Certificate of Occupancy, or C.O., has been issued by the county inspectors certifying that the building is now cleared for occupancy.

There are two types of construction loans. The first, which is structured as shown above, is called a "construction permanent" loan. This is one loan with a single closing that, upon completion of the construction portion, will have an automatic conversion to a regularly amortized payment schedule for the balance of the loan term. The interest rate during construction could be the same after conversion or, it could be modified to a different rate. The repayment during construction is based upon the amount of money actually used, or drawn, by the builder as each pre-specified segment of construction is completed. The consumer is charged only the interest on the amount of money actually drawn during the construction period. Then, at the completion of construction when the C.O. has been issued, the loan is converted into a permanent, regularly amortized loan.

The second is actually two separate loans. The first is called the Construction Loan, and the second is called the End Loan. The construction loan is obtained to fund the actual construction of the building. Upon completion of construction and issuance of the C.O., an "end loan", which is a completely separate loan, is obtained to pay off the construction loan. This end loan is fully amortized and its payments are the equal payments that are usually associated with a mortgage loan. The end loan interest rate, however, often cannot be secured at the time of the first closing. Since the end loan would not begin until construction is completed, this could be six to 12 months following the closing of the construction loan and interest rates fluctuate daily. Generally, the only way to secure the rate for the end loan at the time of the construction loan closing is to pay a premium to guarantee the rate.

Circumstances would dictate which of the two loan types an individual would use. The disadvantage of using the second example is that there are two, completely separate sets of closing costs, one for each loan.

Most people who are building a home would use the construction permanent loan. There is only one closing and, naturally, the closing costs are lower due to that fact. You would need to consult with a mortgage loan professional to determine which is best for your client after considering their individual needs and circumstances.

It is very important that all borrowers are aware that the payment on a construction loan is based on the principle and interest of the loan, plus the taxes and insurance that has been assessed on the property. In order to avoid a major surprise in the year following the completion of construction it is very important to understand that the county will re-compute the property taxes and there will likely be an increase in the escrow account.

The property, when construction began, was being taxed as vacant land which typically has a much lower tax rate. The payments through the end of the calendar year following completion of construction will continue to be based on the vacant land tax rate. However, the subsequent year the county will have reassessed the value of the land and will factor in the new dwelling that is now on it and increase the taxes accordingly. This reassessment will likely mean a significant increase in the property taxes and, consequently, the monthly mortgage payment, if it includes escrows, will go up proportionately. Many lenders or brokers do not make this clear at the closing and the borrower is shocked when they receive their new payment following the tax increase. They find themselves with a payment that could be hundreds of dollars higher and are understandably angry. Please, do not allow this to happen to your clients. Be aware that there will be an increase over the initial mortgage loan payment in subsequent years and inform the borrower.

FIXED RATE LOANS

The fixed rate loan is a mortgage loan on which the interest rate is set at closing and will be fixed for the entire term of the loan. This is the mortgage loan which is the easiest for the ordinary person to understand. The rate is set from the beginning and there are equal payments for the life of the loan. This may fluctuate, however, depending on whether or not their taxes and insurance are escrowed. If the tax or insurance rates change, then the payment will be adjusted accordingly, up or down.

Many people who are seeking a Real Estate mortgage loan want the thirty-year fixed rate and term because it is so easily understood. The problem, however, is that more than 85 percent of people who choose this loan term, end up selling or refinancing their property within three to five years. It is rare for anyone today to stay in the same home beyond five years. During the five years they do remain in that home, they will refinance an average of two times when interest rates change or as their life situation dictates. The bottom line is that they could waste ten thousand dollars or more on interest if they are given ineffective loan guidance.

ADJUSTABLE RATE MORTGAGE (A.R.M.)

In February of 2004, the Chairman of the Federal Reserve, Alan Greenspan, in a speech regarding the state of the economy said that most Americans are making a mistake by taking a 30 year, fixed rate mortgage loan. They would be better served if they considered their situation and the likelihood of remaining in that home for more than five years. An ARM could save thousands of dollars in interest (read spendable income) if they remain in the home five years or less.

He stated that Americans are wasting millions of dollars every year in potentially spendable income. The average American remains in a house between three and five years, yet the vast majority choose a fixed thirty year mortgage loan. It may not be what is best for them, but they get it nonetheless. The main reason for this decision is because they are not made aware of all their options. Most Realtors, Bankers and Mortgage Brokers take the path of least resistance. Rather that educating their borrower/client by explaining their options; they let the borrower settle on that fixed thirty-year, high interest rate mortgage loan.

The Adjustable Rate Mortgage is a very powerful mortgage loan tool. It allows people to obtain a much lower mortgage payment than the traditional thirty-year, fixed rate mortgage loan and can save them thousands of dollars per year in payments and interest.

This type of loan is becoming increasingly popular for many reasons. The principal reason is they are typically one to one and a half percent lower than fixed rate loans. The savings may enable the borrower to afford a higher down payment on their subsequent home purchase and upgrade to a more desirable home. Finding a mortgage specialist who can precisely explain the benefits of a three or five-year fixed rate ARM to a potential buyer is critical to your success. Most people, when shown the savings, will opt for the three or five year fixed rate mortgage loan every time if it has been explained to them accurately.

The following is an example of the difference and savings between a fixed thirty-year mortgage loan and a three year fixed rate loan. ***It is important to understand that the 3 year fixed rate is amortized over a 30 year period.***

$250,000.00 amount financed
30 year fixed rate @ 6.25% note rate = $1,539.29 P&I payment
3 year fixed rate @ 4.875% note rate = $1,323.02 P&I payment

Interest on the 30 year fixed rate note over 36 months = $46,048.67
Interest on the 3 year fixed rate note over 36 months = $35,378.29
Interest saved with 3 year fixed rate note over 36 months = $10,670.38

One of the primary reasons people do not choose adjustable rate mortgages is that most believe that the rate will begin adjusting immediately or, that they are obligated to remain with loan even AFTER the adjustable period begins. This, of course, is not true. *The key to successfully utilizing the 3 year fixed rate is to never let it adjust.* To begin with, the borrower must understand that there are a wide range of ARMs to select from. The monthly adjustable ARMs;

1. The ARM that will begin to adjust on the first month following the closing.
2. The 3 month ARM; this will adjust every 3 months.
3. The 6 month ARM; this will adjust every 6 months.

Then, there are the annual adjustable rate mortgages. Their rates are fixed for the beginning period, which is determined at the beginning of the loan term.

1. The one year ARM, which is fixed for the first year and will adjust according to the index it is based on after the first anniversary of the closing.
2. The 3 year ARM, which is fixed for the first three years and will adjust on the anniversary of the third year after the closing.
3. The five year ARM, which is fixed for the first five years and will adjust on the anniversary of the fifth year following the closing.
4. The seven year ARM, which is fixed for the first seven years and will adjust on the anniversary of the seventh year following the closing.

There are also ten year ARMs but these are, typically, not feasible when compared to the fixed rate loans.

The Adjustable Rate Mortgage is based on an Index pre-selected by the lender. The index can be one of many, depending on who the lender chooses. The index can adjust periodically. The most frequently used indexes are the following:

Treasury Notes
Government Bonds
The Monthly Treasury Average (MTA)
The Cost of Funds Index (COFI)

The Cost of Savings (COSI)
The London Interbank Offered Rate (LIBOR)

While there are others, these are the most common. They have one month, three month, six month, one year, three year, five year, seven year, ten year and thirty year indexes. These indexes are adjusted daily, weekly, monthly or annually, according to lender guidelines and the particular term selected. All of these indexes can be found in the business section of most major newspapers or online at various financial web sites.

The margin is the amount over the index that the borrower will pay to the lender. This is the amount of profit above the index that the lender chooses to make and is preset by the lender prior to closing. The margin is fixed and will not change throughout the entire term of the loan. Both the Index and the Margin should be disclosed as soon as the borrower has selected a loan program and applied for the loan. The margin is commonly 2.25% to 2.75% above the Index but could be higher or lower at the lenders discretion. Many ARMs have an initial starting rate that will be fixed for the initial, pre-specified, fixed rate period of the loan.

For example, let's say today's rate on a 3 year fixed rate ARM based on the LIBOR index is 4.625% and the six month LIBOR index is 1.380%. The margin has been set at 2.75%. Should the index be at the *same level* in 3 years, the rate would adjust to 4.13% at the first scheduled adjustment date. The index of 1.380 PLUS the margin of 2.75 equals the rate of 4.13%. Therefore, the rate would have actually gone *down* and, proportionately, so would the payment.

As you can see from the above examples, the savings with the ARM is considerable. It would give your client more spendable income to use more productively each month.

No wonder Alan Greenspan is promoting the ARM.

It is possible to refinance the ARM into another ARM or a fixed rate mortgage at a future date and pay little, or even no, closing costs.

THE MTA OPTION A.R.M.

(Also know as the Investment Property Vacancy Payment Relief Loan and the Flex Payment Loan)

This particular Adjustable Rate Mortgage requires an explanation all its own. It can be a very powerful mortgage loan tool when it is thoroughly understood and utilized in the appropriate circumstances. The MTA Option ARM is a brilliant mortgage loan option for people investing in property for the short term or for people who require a low starting payment but will be able to afford a higher payment at a later date. It is an ideal tool for the investor, allowing them to maximize their investment while minimizing their expenses. It also has allowances for stated income, which can be an issue for many investors.

The Option ARM is unique in as much as it offers up to four different payment options. The starting rate is very low, producing very low monthly payments. The Option ARM is available at an initial fixed rate period of one month or three months. The actual interest rate adjusts each month after the initial fixed rate period but the pre-set minimum monthly payment adjusts only once a year.

- The borrower can make the minimum monthly payment that adjusts annually. If it is not sufficient to pay the monthly interest then the difference can be deferred up to 115% of the original principal balance. (The borrower can increase the monthly payment and eliminate the deferred interest that may have accrued or the borrower may pay the deferred interest in a lump sum at any time)
- The borrower can increase the payment to include all of the interest due, thereby avoiding a negative amortization.
- The borrower can pay the fully amortized payment, which would include the actual interest due and a principal reduction based on a 30 year term.
- The borrower can pay the fully amortized payment based on a 15 year term.

The interest rate on this loan has an index based on the MTA, or twelve-month average of monthly yields on actively traded U.S. Treasury securities, adjusted to a constant maturity of one year. The average is calculated every month and based on the previous twelve months activity.

One of this program's most financially beneficial features is that the very low starting payment is guaranteed for twelve months. At the end of that time, the payment is adjusted, but it cannot go up more than 7.5% from where it started. Using the same $250,000 mortgage loan amount that we used in the original ARM calculation, the initial, minimum payment would be; $804.10. This is based on an initial minimum note rate of one percent. The actual, fully indexed note rate would be 4.75%. The following year, the minimum monthly payment would go up by 7.5% which would amount to a payment of; $864.41 per month, a $60.31 increase. Then, this new minimum payment is guaranteed for the next twelve months.
The following year, the payment could not go up more than $864.41. X 7.5% = $64.83 = new payment of $929.24 which would remain at that amount for the rest of that year. So, by the end of three years, the most the payment could have gone up is $125.14. This is a controlled increase so as not to be a shock to the borrower if rates have climbed. This same formula is applicable for the first five years.

If the minimum payment is what the borrower chooses to make, the loan may then become "negative amortization." This is due to the fact that by making the minimum payment only, all of the interest due may not have been paid. If there is a negative interest balance it is added back to the principle of the loan amount.

Should the borrower have chosen to pay the interest portion of the required payment, then the loan would NOT go negative amortization. The payment would be based on the fully indexed rate of 4.75% which was the actual interest rate at the beginning of the loan. The interest only payment on $250,000.00 would be $987.50. It should be noted that when comparing this to a fixed, thirty-year note at 6.25% which would have a payment of $1,539.29, the Option ARM is offering a monthly savings of $725.29, based on the minimum payment. The interest only payment would be $989.58, a monthly savings of $549.71.

Most borrowers, who believe they will be in the home for approximately three to five years, will realize a payment savings of $26,110.44 over the three years when making only the minimum payment and $19,789.56 when making the interest only payment. No matter how you look at it, this is a very substantial monthly payment savings. This savings, coupled with the appreciation they will realize after three years will, of course, mean that they will net a significant amount of money to put down on their next home. Of course, as the Realtor primarily responsible for this savings, you will be high on their list of people to contact when they are ready to purchase that next home.

Also, there is the fact that, with most lenders who offer this program, the highest the Option ARM interest rate can ever go is to 9.5%. When compared to the 5/1 ARM or the 3/1 ARM it actually has a lower lifetime cap. The cap on the 5/1 ARM is six percent above the starting rate. The starting rate as of July 30th, 2004 was 5.25%. This means that the lifetime cap on the 5/1 ARM would be 11.25% or 2.34% *higher* than the lifetime cap on the Option ARM. The 3/1 ARM is 4.75%, which means the life cap would be 10.75% or 1.85% *higher* than the Option ARM.

You can see how the Option ARM, or Investor Vacancy Payment Relief Loan, or Flex Option Payment Loan, however it is labeled, could truly benefit a prospect whose financial circumstances allowed for this type of loan program.

It is called the Investor Vacancy Payment Relief Loan because if the situation should call for a minimal payment, the option exists. Should the borrower be an investor who rents the property and it becomes vacant, the cash flow dries up. With the Vacancy Payment Relief Loan, the investor would only have to make the minimum payment. This would minimize the mortgage payment expense as much as possible under the circumstances. Once the cash flow resumes, the investor could increase the payment to the interest only or fully amortized amount if he chooses to do so.

THE 80/20 and 80/10/10 LOAN
(100% LTV and avoid PMI)

This type of loan is commonly the only way to obtain a 100% LTV conventional mortgage loan without paying the PMI insurance. The fact is there are actually two separate loans, usually with a single lender. Here is the way it works: there is an eighty percent LTV first mortgage and a twenty percent LTV second mortgage. The first mortgage can be either a fixed rate and term loan or an ARM. The second can be a HELOC or a fixed rate and term equity loan. The combined loan to value is usually an 80-20, for one hundred percent combined loan to value (CLTV). It may also be an 80-10-10, where the borrower puts up ten percent of their own funds with an 80% first and a 10% second mortgage. This scenario may be worked in different combinations, such as a 75-20-5 or an 80-15-5, etc.

The key to avoiding the PMI is to have no more than 80% on the first mortgage. The interest rate on the first mortgage loan portion of an 80-20 will almost always be lower than on a single 90% LTV loan. The interest rate on the second is generally very reasonable with the payment being based on interest only. (With the option of paying more, of course.)

When structured properly, the 80-10-10 may result in a payment hundreds of dollars lower than a single loan of 90% with PMI.

I obtain mortgage loans for many people who are clients of major banks. These people will go to their banks for a mortgage loan equaling 90% of the selling price and the bank loan officer will simply take an application and put them into a single 90% LTV loan with PMI. That is the way the average loan officer has been trained.

When given the opportunity to speak with these people, I've been able to show them proof that the 80-10-10 can save more than one hundred dollars per month in PMI and have a lower interest rate on the first mortgage. It will also result in an overall lower payment even though there are two separate loans. Most of the folks to whom I've shown this program have financed their homes with me. It's simply a matter of using creativity to structure the loan in a manner that is most advantageous to the client.

NO INCOME VERIFICATION

This type of loan is also commonly known as the N.I.V. loan, the No Ratio loan, and the No Doc loan. It is very important to understand that these are actually three distinctly different types of loans. They are frequently confused by borrowers and originators alike. It is very important to understand the differences between each because they must be structured differently. Once the loan file has been structured and submitted, if it turns out to be incorrect in any way, it cannot be changed from an N.I.V. to No Ratio or No Doc without changing lenders and starting all over. Once the underwriter has seen the file including the income or any other facts as originally submitted those items cannot be removed from the file or changed. The result of an error of structuring could, of course, lead to the lender being unable to underwrite the file as submitted thereby jeopardizing the closing and, perhaps, the entire transaction.

The No Income Verification, also known as a stated income loan, means that the income is listed on the application, but is *not verified* with W-2's, pay-stubs, or tax returns. The income stated must be reasonable for the profession and be consistent with accumulated assets and credit history. It is important to understand that the assets *will* be listed on the application and *must be verified with bank statements and other related account statements.* This type of loan is particularly good for people who are self employed and, due to accounting techniques, do not show much personal income on their returns.

The No Ratio loan means that the income is not listed on the application at all. It is mandatory that employment be disclosed for a period of twenty-four to forty-eight months, depending on the LTV of the property being purchased. Employment and income sources must be of a type that could reasonably support the ability to repay the loan. Just as with the No Income Verification loan, the assets must be listed and verified.

The true No Doc (no documentation) loan is a loan where the employment, income and assets *are not listed on the application at all.*

It is important to understand that all three of these loans are dependent on credit scores and that all three have different interest rates and loan to value (LTV) allowances.

The N.I.V. loan would have the most flexibility in terms of credit score requirements. For example, this type of loan may be available in the sub-prime market with credit score allowances down to 580 with an LTV of 90%. Remember, the lower the credit scores, the higher the rate. However, if a person has high credit scores, the LTV can go up to 100% and have very attractive interest rates. The interest rate on the NIV loan is typically only one eighth to one quarter percent higher than a fully documented loan.

The No Ratio loan is useful in a situation where the credit scores are good and a higher LTV is required, but the parameters of the NIV loan will not work. The rate will be higher than the N.I.V. loan. Typically, the credit scores on the No Ratio Loan will need to be above 680 for an 80% LTV and above 700 for a higher LTV. There can be no foreclosures or bankruptcy history for more than seven years prior to application. The interest rate on this type of loan would be approximately one quarter to one half percent higher than the fully documented loan.

The No Documentation loan would require very good credit scores, a minimum of 680, depending on the LTV. The LTV would generally be limited to 90% at best. The interest rate on this type of loan would be approximately one half to one percent higher than the fully documented loan. The fact that the credit scores are very good does not mean that the rate will be low. This is considered a very high risk loan due to the fact that nothing, i.e., income, assets, or employment, is being verified in any way. The credit is being extended based almost exclusively on the credit score and history.

Keep in mind that on all loans, from a lender and underwriters viewpoint, the higher the risk, the higher the rate.

FOREIGN NATIONAL LOANS

Foreign Nationals are people who maintain a non-resident alien status. Some non-resident aliens have obtained a "Green Card" (which is now know as an Alien Registration Receipt Card) and have certain additional rights and privileges as regards mortgage financing. These are considered "Resident Aliens. These Green Card resident aliens can obtain a mortgage loan just the same as if they were citizens. The true Foreign National typically has a visa to stay in the United States for a limited period of time. They may own property in the U.S. and frequently purchase vacation homes or second homes in the U.S. while maintaining their primary residence and career in another country.

There are lenders or investors in the U.S.A. who will accept foreign credit reports and income verification. They will accept letters of recommendation, credit and asset verification from Foreign Banks. There are Foreign National loan programs and portfolio programs designed to meet the needs of Foreign National and Non-Permanent Resident Aliens who do not meet the two year eligibility requirements of residency, employment and credit. Typically, the programs allow for between 70 and 80% LTV with no American Credit history what-so-ever. Some lenders do, however, require a limited or minimal American credit history. If foreign credit is allowed usually a letter from a foreign bank verifying the character of the applicant borrower, statements verifying assets and credit history will generally satisfy underwriting requirements. The maximum allowable LTV on Foreign National loans is 80% providing the aforementioned criteria have been met. Also, the subject property must be an owner occupied residence, not an investment property.

NON-CONVENTIONAL & SUB-PRIME LOANS

These terms describe certain types of loans that do not fit into or meet the underwriting requirements of traditional, or conventional, loans. The reasons for this may vary, but it typically describes borrowers who have moderate to severe credit issues or those who cannot verify part, or all, of their income. Non-conventional also describes Home Equity loans. While home equity loans are commonly extended to borrowers with good credit, they are in second position behind a first mortgage and are not sold through the secondary market resulting in their non-conventional status.

However, for our purpose here, we are referring to Non-conventional or Sub-prime loans, sometimes called B, C, and D credit loans, typically used for people who have had moderate to severe issues in their credit history. These issues could be slow pay, or late payments, collections, liens, judgments, bankruptcy, repossessions or real estate foreclosures. As bad as these sound, there is almost always a way to obtain financing for clients with severe credit issues. Non-conventional loans are also used for people who cannot verify their income, assets, or both. There are non-conventional lenders and investors who will even extend loans to people who are not employed at all. Another scenario would be property that is considered non-conventional. One example of this would be condominiums that are still in the development stage and are considered non-warrantable by Fannie Mae standards. This means that there are limited buyers for this type of real estate loan on the secondary market, making it more difficult for investors to sell the loan. People with debt-to-income ratios that exceed acceptable Fannie Mae guidelines are also considered non-conventional.

It is very important for the Loan Originator to understand that non-conforming and sub-prime loans now constitute more than 50% of all home mortgage loans. You don't want to miss a sale just because you find out that someone has credit issues, low scores or has no way to verify their income and/or assets.

If the issues are credit related and we have an explanation that may show a catastrophic incident, such as illness, injury, divorce, or the like is what caused the problems, we may be able to structure the loan for a non-conventional investor and obtain a more favorable interest rate. Some lenders or investors will allow for mortgage late payments, collections and even charged off accounts and still go as high as 100% LTV.

In most instances, the interest rate for a non-conventional loan is going to be higher than conventional interest rates. The client will be considered a higher risk due to the credit history or inability to verify his income. However, by using a two or three year fixed rate ARM program, we may be able to offer a loan with a rate and payment that is comparable to a fixed rate, conventional mortgage. We call these sub-prime ARM loans that are fixed for the first one or two years, "Band Aide" loans. This is because they are rarely kept to full term and are paid off or refinanced after the fixed rate period has ended. The "Band Aide" loan allows the borrower to accomplish their goal of purchasing real estate at today's prices while giving them time to get their credit issues straightened out or their income situation stabilized to where it may be verified. Once these goals have been accomplished the "Band Aide" loan may be refinanced to a conventional loan with a more beneficial interest rate.

Most lenders and investors realize that the borrower is obtaining this loan for the short term and charge a higher interest rate. They need to be able to make these loans profitable in order to continue this lending practice. The investor or lender will commonly assure this profit by charging a pre-payment penalty. Typically, the term of this penalty is 12 to 36 months and is not generally an objection for most borrowers. The borrower understands that it will take at least that long to re-establish an acceptable credit score or to arrange for their income to become stable and verifiable. Many reputable lenders or brokers will work with the borrower to refinance the original loan to a lower rate and payment while charging reduced closing costs.

CREDIT SCORING AND CREDIT ISSUES

This area that remains a mystery to many loan officers and bankers, due to the fact that they have never been educated to understand how credit scores are arrived at. It is not a mystery at all. A responsible loan officer will have taken the time to research the system, learn how it works and know how to advise his clients should they have low credit scores or credit related issues. It is important to know that not all low credit scores are indicative of credit problems. A professional mortgage broker will advise his clients what they can do to raise their scores if they are low. (Most bankers are not allowed to credit counsel their clients.) He will know, understand and be able to interpret the reports for the client and give them appropriate guidance. Remember, "There is a way to obtain a mortgage *if* you know how to structure the loan." Interpreting a credit report is a key element of the loan structure.

What is a Credit Bureau Score, and how is it calculated?

Credit bureau scoring is a statistical means of assessing how likely a borrower is to pay back a loan. A Credit Bureau Score is based on the data available in the borrower's credit report. The score measures the relative degree of risk a potential borrower represents to the lender or investor. It is not a measure of a borrower's income, assets, or bank account, although those and other factors are still considered by lenders and investors, independent of the score. A Credit Bureau Score does not include any of the following in the score calculation as this would be discriminatory by FCRA guidelines: gender, race, age, or ZIP Code.

Fair, Isaacs Credit Bureau Scores range from approximately 300 to 900 points, and are available through the three national credit data repositories (Equifax, Trans Union, and Experian). The scoring programs reside at these credit bureaus and are called:

BEACON	at	EQUIFAX
EMPIRICA	at	TRANS UNION
Experian/Fair, Isaacs Model	at	EXPERIAN

This score is calculated at the repository, and is based solely on the data within that repository's individual credit file. Fair, Isaac is not able to access a borrower's credit data or calculate a score.
A Fair, Isaac Credit Bureau Score, sometimes referred to as the "FICO" score, is calculated by a system of scorecards. In developing these scorecards, Fair, Isaac uses actual credit data on millions of consumers, and applies complex mathematical methods to perform extensive research into credit patterns that forecast credit performance. Through this process, Fair, Isaac identifies distinctive credit patterns. Each pattern corresponds to the likelihood that a consumer will make his or her loan payments as agreed in the future. The score is based on all the credit-related data in the credit bureau

report; not just negative data such as missed mortgage payments or bankruptcies.

Although the FICO scores are helpful in predicting the likelihood of default, their main purpose is to predict loan delinquency. If loan default is the focus of your scoring objectives, you should investigate bankruptcy scores.

The types of credit information used in the credit bureau scorecards are typically the same items an underwriter would use to make a credit decision. These can include:

PAYMENT HISTORY

- Public record and collection items
- Severity, recentness, and frequency of delinquencies noted in trade line section

OUTSTANDING DEBT

- Number of balances recently reported
- Average balance across all trade lines
- Relationship between total balances and total credit limits on revolving trade line
  (This is *typically* the number one reason for low scores)

CREDIT HISTORY

- Age of oldest trade line
- Number of new trade lines

PURSUIT OF NEW CREDIT

- Number of inquiries and new account openings in the last year
  (Each new inquiry counts for 3 to 5 points off of score)
- Amount of time since most recent inquiry

TYPES OF CREDIT IN USE

- Number of trade lines reported for each of the following types:

1. Bankcard
2. Travel and Entertainment cards

3. Department store cards
4. Personal finance company references
5. Installment loans
6. Other

UNDERSTANDING THE CREDIT BUREAU SCORE

A FICO score is a means of rank-ordering potential borrowers based on the likelihood that they will pay their credit obligations as agreed. A higher score indicates better credit quality. If all other things are equal, borrowers with a score of 660, for example, are less likely to default on a loan than borrowers with a score of 650. It is factored that close.

CREDIT SCORE RANGES FOR NEW MORTGAGE BORROWERS FROM A NATIONAL SAMPLE

SCORE RANGE showing the number of good loans for each bad loan showing serious delinquency or foreclosures:

	(Ratio of good loans to one bad)
Below 600	8 to 1
700-719	123 to 1
Above 800	1,292 to 1

The following are the top reasons why a credit report scored the way it did.

1. Delinquency on accounts
2. Amount owed on accounts is too high
3. Too many accounts opened in the last 12 months
4. Too few accounts currently paid as agreed
5. Judgments or Liens

These score factor explanations can be relayed back to the borrower to explain how they can increase their score over time. The key, of course, is for the loan officer who pulled the credit report to understand the score factors and present the findings knowledgeably and effectively back to the borrower.

"Time heals all wounds." We've all heard that enduring bit of wisdom spoken at one time or another. It is true of credit issues, too. The older the issue, the less weight it carries. This, however, does not apply to such issues as tax liens or judgments.

USING EQUITY FROM EXISTING PROPERTY

This program is for a person who wants to buy a new home now, but has to wait for his existing home to sell because that is the source of his down payment.

This program is not for everyone, but can work very well for people who have considerable equity in their existing home and have good credit. The equity may also be in another property, such as an investment property, vacation home, second home or even a commercial property.

The key is for the loan officer to understand how to structure the loan so that the buyer can take out the equity in their existing property, pay only interest on that loan (assuring a low payment) for up to 10 years, and still buy the new property. When used correctly, this is a very powerful tool that will result in an immediate sale with no contingencies. In the past, a bridge loan was the only way to accomplish this but most investors and banks no longer offer bridge loans. If the loan officer understands how to correctly structure the loans the equity loan will be fast, easy and with little or, sometimes no, closing costs.

The client will then have up to ten years to sell their existing home and pay off the equity line. The bridge loan program gives them a maximum of two years.

DOCUMENTS TYPICALLY REQUIRED AT APPLICATION

In the case of most loan applications, when the loan is going to require full documentation, lenders typically require the same items. The following is a list of the "standard" documents needed.

1. Most recent two years W-2's
2. Most recent pay-stubs
3. Last 3 months of bank statements
4. All statements from stocks, bonds, 401K, IRA, or retirement accounts when used as an asset to show ability to procure down payment.
5. Award letter from Social Security if that is their source of income
6. Last two years of tax returns (if self employed)
7. Divorce decree if child support is being used as income

In the case of a stated income loan, only items three and four will be required.

An experienced loan officer will know when any, or all, of these items will be required as he begins to structure the loan program to fit the clients needs and requirements.

CLOSING PROCEDURES

1. Have the client bring in a cashier's check for the down payment and closing costs, if required.
2. Bring a photo i.d.
3. The closing agent will review the documents to assure accuracy. *The loan officer or loan originator should be there to make certain that the interest rate and loan terms are what were agreed upon.*
4. The loan will fund shortly after all of the documents have been signed and completed.

THE AGE OF SPECIALIZATION

In this age of specialization it is important to do just that; specialize in your field. Realtors who specialize in listing, showing and selling Real Estate spend many hours training and are certified, sometimes at multiple levels, as professionals in that field. When a Realtor is writing a contract, through asking the proper questions, they will determine if the client may require mortgage financing assistance. If the Realtor received the proper training regarding mortgage loan financing they will have at least a rudimentary understanding of their clients needs. After asking basic, qualifying questions, the experienced Real Estate Professional will know when to refer their client to a Mortgage Loan Professional, who they are certain has the proper professional training and experience. The Mortgage Loan Professional will ask the appropriate questions, accurately determine their client's needs, and have the mortgage product base to meet those needs. The competent Mortgage Loan Professional will know how to structure the loan to best serve that client's situation, ultimately resulting in a smooth, overall transaction and closing. The client will appreciate the Realtor's referral to a qualified Mortgage Loan Professional and the Realtor will have very little stress associated with the transaction. The end result will guarantee a continuous stream of referrals from satisfied clients.

It is essential for the Realtor to understand that not all Mortgage Loan Originators know how to correctly structure a loan and where to place that loan to assure an approval. It is unfortunate, but true, that many Mortgage Loan Originators did not receive adequate basic training and are forced to learn on the job. You do not want to be one of the under educated or inexperienced Mortgage Originators who are learning at the expense of the client, and who could potentially jeopardize the entire transaction. Become a true specialist in the mortgage field. Earn the confidence of your Realtors so they will refer all of their prospective buyers to you. You will be *the* loan specialist, the trusted partner who inspires confidence through successful loan placement and timely closings. You will become an extension of the Realtors business and the referrals will become automatic.

Recently, one of the many Realtors who refer business to me had a client who almost cancelled the transaction just two weeks before the scheduled closing. For some reason this particular Realtor always gives the buyer three choices of different lenders and loan officers. I was one choice; however the buyer decided to use a loan officer with a bank whose brand name he recognized. He made application and was given a rate and term. Over the next three weeks, he realized that he had not been given a very good rate and term. He would be paying mortgage insurance financing 90% of the value of the house being purchased, and his payment would be higher than expected. He was on the verge of canceling the entire transaction and forfeiting his deposit. He realized that as his taxes or insurance increased he would risk not being able to make his payments.

Fortunately, the client called me at the eleventh hour, less than two weeks prior to the scheduled closing. Upon receiving an application from him and obtaining his credit report, I found that I could save him a full half of a percent on the mortgage rate. I also combined his first mortgage with a simultaneously closing, purchase money second mortgage to avoid the PMI. The net result was a lower rate, his payment was reduced by over one hundred dollars per month and he had no PMI. It was simply a matter of understanding his needs and creatively structuring a loan program that would meet those needs. Bottom line: the loan closed on time and the client was very pleased with his Realtor and his mortgage loan. The Realtor will be receiving many referrals from that client in the future, and I will be receiving many referrals from that Realtor.

I have been called upon, time and again, to clean up problems from a previous loan originator who did not necessarily have the client's best interests in mind or did not know how to correctly structure the loan. Learn your trade well and become the "Go to" mortgage broker in your market.

THE VALUE OF A MORTGAGE BROKER

(Quoted from the National Association of Mortgage Brokers)

"According to a 2003 study by Wholesale Access Mortgage Research & Consulting, Inc., there are approximately 44,000 mortgage brokerage companies that employ an estimated 360,000 loan officers and ***originate more than 65% of all residential loans in the U.S.*** The mortgage broker industry is regulated by 10 federal laws, five federal enforcement agencies and over 45 state laws or licensing boards.

Mortgage brokers are real estate financing professionals acting as the intermediary between consumers and lenders during mortgage transactions. A mortgage broker works with consumers to help them through the complex mortgage origination process.

A typical broker has a working relationship with numerous banks and other lenders and provides the consumer with access to hundreds of options when it comes to financing a home. This allows mortgage brokers to provide consumers the most efficient and cost-effective method of obtaining the mortgage that fits the consumer's financial goals and circumstances. Mortgage brokers have helped many consumers, including low-to-moderate income borrowers with less than perfect credit histories, enjoy the benefits of homeownership."

FOOD FOR THOUGHT

Without exception, all Mortgage Brokers who have read this book or taken our class *and* utilized the information they've learned as a result, *and* have developed a working relationship with their own group of Realtors, title companies, and property appraisers, have increased their sales and closings.

Without exception.

MORTGAGE BANKING GLOSSARY

Adjustable Rate Mortgage (ARM)

A mortgage in which the interest rate is adjusted periodically according to a pre-selected index.

Amortization

Repayment of a loan by equal payments to retire the principal at the end of a fixed term, to pay accrued interest on the outstanding balance.

Amortization Schedule

A table showing the amounts of principal and interest due at regular intervals and the unpaid balance of the loan after each payment is made.

Annual Percentage rate

Cost of credit as calculated according to the consumer protection act (Regulation Z). APR includes the stated interest rate on the loan plus all additional finance charges associated with the loan. (i.e., points, mortgage insurance, broker fees, etc.)

Appraisal

A report made by a licensed, qualified person setting forth an opinion or estimates of value. The term also refers to the process by which this estimate is obtained.

Appreciation

An increase in value.

Arrears

The opposite of "in advance". The situation in which mortgage interest and real estate taxes are paid at or after the end of the period or year for which they are due. Also, the state of being delinquent or behind in paying a debt.

Assignment

The transfer of a right or contract from one person, or entity, to another.

Assumption

A written agreement by one party to pay an obligation originally incurred by another.

Balloon Mortgage

A mortgage with periodic installments of principal and interest that do not fully amortize the loan. The balance of the mortgage is due in a lump sum at a specified date in the future, usually at the end of the term.

Bankrupt

Being relieved from payment of all debts after the surrender of all assets. Chapter 7- liquidation of debtor's assets; Chapter 11 – reorganization of business; Chapter 13 – repayment schedule established through the courts.

Base Loan Amount

The current principal balance minus the MIP refund.

Basis Point

One one-hundredth of one percent. Used to describe the amount of change in yield in many debt instruments, including mortgages.

Bi-Weekly Mortgage

With a standard 30-year mortgage, borrowers pay off their loan by making 12 monthly payments yearly. The bi-weekly mortgage requires one more monthly payment yearly – 13 instead of 12 – but with payments being made every two weeks instead of every month. This results in 26 payments a year, with the mortgage being paid off in 18 or 19 years.

Buy down

Money advanced by an individual (builder, seller, etc.) to reduce the monthly payments for a home mortgage either during the entire term or for an initial period of years.

Clear Title

Title not encumbered or burdened with defects.

Closing

The conclusion of a transaction. Delivery of a deed, signing of a note and the disbursement of funds.

Closing Costs

The money paid by borrowers to effect the closing of a mortgage loan. May include origination fee, discount points, title insurance and survey among others.

Collateral

Property pledged as security for a debt. In the case of default, the lenders claim to that property is exercised to satisfy the debt.

Co-Mortgagor

A person appearing on the application with the mortgagor. Their income, assets, and debts are combined with the mortgagor for underwriting and ratio analysis.

Condominium

Fee ownership of a unit of space in developed realty plus an undivided interest in common areas owned jointly with others in the same development.

Conventional Loan

A mortgage loan not insured by the government

Co-Signer

An individual who is individually and jointly liable for repayment of a debt but has no ownership interest.

Cost Options

With traditional refinancing the borrower has the ability to buy down to a lower interest rate.

Coupon Book

A payment book containing coupons which the borrower sends every month to his lender along with his mortgage check. The book also contains an escrow analysis, providing the amount of monthly tax and insurance deposits the borrower is required to pay.

Deed of Trust

An instrument which secures a note. It conveys an interest in the property to a third party and is recorded with the county. A Deed of Trust DOES NOT CONVEY TITLE TO

THE PROPERTY. May also be referred to as a Mortgage Deed depending on state Real Estate Laws.

Default

Failure to honor the terms of a loan contract or note.

Delayed Disbursement

A method of disbursement which allows a borrower to close early in the month and pay interest as though the loan closed at the end of the month.

Delinquency

Failure to make timely payments under a loan agreement.

Depreciation

A loss in value.

Direct Endorsement

An FHA program that enables an eligible single family lender to conduct the processing, approval and closing of an FHA loan without HUD'S prior approval.

Discount Point

An amount based on the loan amount paid to the lender to cover the cost of funds, usually lowering the interest rate. A point is equal to 1% of the loan amount. (This will affect APR)

Discount Rate

In central banking, the rate the Federal Reserve charges to member banks that borrow money from it.

Down Payment

The difference between the sales price and the mortgage amount.

Duplex

A single structure designed with two separate housing units.

Easement

The right or privilege to use the land of another for a specific purpose such as a driveway or maintenance of power lines.

ECOA

Equal Credit Opportunity Act – A federal law that requires lenders to make credit equally available without discrimination based on race, color, religion, national origin, age, sex, or marital status.

Encroachment

An improvement that illegally trespasses on another's property.

Encumbrance

Anything that affects or limits the fee simple title to property, such as mortgages, leases, easements, judgments or restrictions.

Equity

The difference between the market value of a property and the balance of the loans against it usually referred to as the owner's interest.

Escrow Analysis

An annual accounting of the monies collected and paid out in relation to the property taxes, hazard insurance and mortgage insurance.

Escrow Payment

The portion of a mortgagor's monthly payments held by the lender or loan servicer to pay taxes and insurance premiums.

Federal Home Loan Mortgage Corporation

A secondary Market agency of the Federal Home Loan Bank which buys and sells Conventional Loans. (Freddie Mac or FHLMC)

Federal Housing Administration (FHA)

A division of the Department of Housing and Urban Development (HUD) which insures mortgage loans made by lenders who comply with certain underwriting and construction standards.

Federal National Mortgage Association

A private Secondary Market agency created by Congress which buys and sells both Conventional and Government loans. (Fannie Mae)

Fee Simple

The most complete form of ownership in real estate which includes all rights and privileges.

First Mortgage

A real estate loan that creates a primary lien against real property.

Fixed Rate Mortgage

A mortgage on which the interest rate is set for the term of the loan.

Flood Plain

Those lands subject to flooding.

Forbearance

Refraining from taking legal action despite the fact that the mortgage is in arrears. Usually granted only when a mortgagor makes arrangements by which the arrears will be paid at a future date.

Good Faith Estimate

In compliance with the Real Estate Settlement Procedures Act, the GFE discloses to the borrower all of the costs associated with the loan transaction. The Good Faith Estimate discloses the interest rate and settlement charges in effect on the date of application.

Government National Mortgage Association (GNMA)

A Secondary Market agency supervised by HUD that issues securities backed by Government loans. GNMA securities are subject to GNMA and PSA regulations.

Grace Period

A specified period after the due date of a payment before a late charge is assessed, (usually 15 days on a mortgage loan).

Graduated Payment Mortgage (GPM)

A type of flexible payment mortgage where payments increase for a specified period of time and then level off.

Grantee

The person to whom an interest in real property is conveyed.

Hazard Insurance

A form of insurance coverage for real estate which compensates the owner for losses caused by fire, certain natural causes, vandalism and theft.

Home Equity Loan

Second mortgage financing that consists of a fixed rate with an amortized payment based on a ten or fifteen year period, that is secured by the appraised market value of the property and is typically used for a specified purpose.

Home Equity Line of Credit (HELOC)

Second mortgage financing that consists of a revolving line of credit with an adjustable rate that is secured by the appraised market value of the property and is usable for any purpose. Typically, funds from the HELOC can be drawn upon for a ten year period after which time the rate becomes fixed, the funds no longer be drawn, and an additional five year period is given for repayment.

Homeowners Association (HOA)

An organization of property owners within a development whose purpose is to maintain and provide community facilities. It has the power to collect dues or assessments; HOA's are usually found in connection with Condo projects or PUD's (Planned Unit Developments).

HUD (Dept of Housing and Urban Development)

A cabinet department of the federal government responsible for federal housing and urban development programs. It governs FHA and GNMA operations.

Investor

The holder of a mortgage or the permanent lender for whom the mortgage banker services the loan; any person or institution that invests in mortgages.

Joint Tenancy

Joint ownership by two or more persons giving each tenant equal interest and equal rights in the property.

Judgment

A court decree of indebtedness to another. May create a lien against property owned.

Kickback

Payment in return for the referral of a client, customer, or business. Kickbacks are a direct violation of RESPA laws.

Late Charge

When the borrowers mortgage payment is received by the lender more than 15 days late, they will be assessed a penalty equaling 5% of the total mortgage payment.

Legal Description

A specific and unique identification of a parcel of real estate that is recognized and approved by law.

Lien

A legal hold or claim of one person on the property of another as security for a debt.

Loan to Value Ratio (LTV)

The relationship of the loan amount to the appraised value of the property.

Locked-In

A written guarantee by the lender that a borrower will close at a specific interest rate.

Market Rate

The interest rate that one can obtain without paying any discount points, but will be required to pay closing costs.

Market Value

The highest price which a property should bring in a competitive and open market not affected by undue stimulus. Where buyer and seller are both informed and motivated. Usually determined by an appraisal.

Maturity Date

The date on which the note or agreement expires. The date that last payment is due.

Mortgage

A legal document which pledges real property as security for a loan. (See Deed of Trust)

Mortgage Backed Securities

Bond-type investment securities representing an individual interest in a pool of mortgages of trust deeds. Income from underlying mortgages is used to pay off the securities.

Mortgage Banker

A firm or individual who originates loans for sale to other investors. The mortgage banker generally continues to service the loans.

Mortgage Broker

A firm or individual who brings the borrower and the lender together, receiving commission if a sale results. A mortgage broker does not retain servicing.

Mortgage Insurance Premium (MIP)

The amount paid by a mortgagor for mortgage insurance either to FHA (FHA loans) or a private mortgage insurance company (conventional loans) which covers a percentage of loss due to default.

Mortgage Loan

A loan secured by real property.

Mortgage Note

A written promise to pay a sum of money at a stated interest rate during a specified term, which is secured by a mortgage.

Mortgagee

The lender in a mortgage transaction.

Mortgagee Clause

A Hazard Insurance policy provision for payment of a claim to someone (the lender) other than the insured, for damages to the property.

Mortgagor

The borrower in a mortgage transaction.

Negative Amortization

A loan payment schedule which causes the outstanding principal balance to increase because the payments are not sufficient to cover the full amount of interest due. The unpaid interest is added to the principal.

Origination Fee

The amount charged by a lender to process and prepare loan documents. Usually computed as a percentage of the loan amount.

Originator

A person who solicits others to obtain applications for mortgage loans.

Payment History

A statement from a borrower's current lender showing when mortgage payments were received. Most investors require the most recent twelve-month payment history in which a borrower can be no more than 3 times 30 days late.

Pipeline

Term used to express loan applications in process up until closing.

PITI

Principal, Interest, Taxes and Insurance.

Planned Unit Development (PUD)

A development which allows greater overall density than usual but containing open and common areas in between.

Plat

A map representing a piece of land subdivided into lots with streets, boundaries and easements shown.

Point

An amount equal to one percent of the loan amount. Loan discount points are a one-time charge assessed at closing by the lender to increase the yield on the mortgage loan.

Power of Attorney

A legal document which authorizes one person to act on behalf of another.

Preliminary HUD

A statement communicating the details of a loan transaction. It consists of previous loan information, closing requirements and a detailed projection of closing figures.

Prepaid Interest

Mortgage interest that is paid in advance of when it is due.

Prepaids

The amount necessary to cover interest to the date of first payment, the initial hazard insurance premium and fees to cover the cost of loan origination.

Prepayment

The act of paying off a loan before the end of its term by making additional payments to the required mortgage payment. There are no prepayment penalties on most Fannie Mae and Freddie Mac loans.

Prime Rate

The interest rate that banks charge to their most preferred customers. It tends to be the yardstick for general trends in interest rates.

Quality Application

An application taken from a committed client that is thoroughly completed without math errors, spelling errors or missing documentation.

Qualifying Assumption

A type of loan assumption that requires the purchaser to qualify just like he would on a new loan.

Quit Claim Deed

A deed by which the owner of real estate conveys their interest to another but makes no representation that the property is free from encumbrances.

Recording

Entering legal documents into the public record thereby giving constructive notice to all interests involved.

Refinance

The repayment of a debt from the proceeds of a new loan using the same property as security.

Regulation Z

The title of the Federal Reserve Board's ruling implementing the Consumer Credit Protection Act. (See Truth in Lending)

Release of Liability

An agreement by a lender to terminate the personal obligation of a mortgagor in connection with the payment of a debt.

Rescission

The act of rescinding or canceling a transaction. Borrowers receives three full business days after closing to cancel his loan if he, or she, chooses to do so when the subject property is the borrower's primary residence. (Florida)

RESPA (Real Estate Settlement Procedures Act)

A law enacted in June of 1976 which requires lenders to provide mortgage borrowers with information of known or estimated settlement costs.

Seasoning

The maturing of a mortgage; the length of time that has passed since closing.

Second Mortgage

A mortgage that has rights secondary to the first mortgage.

Secondary Mortgage Market

A system whereby lenders and investors buy existing mortgages or mortgage-backed securities, and in doing so, provide greater availability of funds for additional mortgage lending by bankers, mortgagee bankers and S & L's.

Servicing

The administration and collection of payments.

Settlement Costs

Money paid by borrowers and sellers to affect the closing of a mortgage loan. This normally includes an origination fee, discount points, title insurance, etc.

Subordination

The act of a party acknowledging that a debt is inferior to the interest of another in the same property.

Survey

A measurement of land prepared by a registered land surveyor.

Title

Evidence of the right to or ownership in property.

Title Insurance Policy

A contract by which the insurer agrees to pay the insured a specific amount of any loss caused by defects of title to real estate, wherein the insured has an interest as purchaser, mortgagee, or otherwise.

Truth in Lending (TIL)

Popular name for the Consumer Credit Protection Act of 1968 which requires lenders to fully disclose credit terms, conditions, the APR, and other charges in writing. Used synonymously with Reg-Z. This was designed to show the cost of credit over a specific period of time.

Underwriting

An analysis of risk involving the determination of a borrower's ability and willingness to repay the loan.

Variable Rate Mortgage

A mortgage agreement that allows for adjustment of the interest rate in keeping with a fluctuating market and terms agreed upon in the note.

Verification of Deposit (VOD)

The form that is used to determine the amount of funds the borrower has on deposit and available for use.

Warranty Deed

The instrument which transfers title and guarantees that the grantor has clear and unencumbered title to the property.